visual **writing**

visual writing

Anne Hanson

LEARNINGEXPRESS

NEW YORK

Printed in the United States of America

Library of Congress Cataloging-in-Publication Data:
Hanson, Anne, 1950-
    Visual writing / by Anne Hanson—1st ed.
      p.cm
    ISBN 1-57685-405-1
    1. English language—Rhetoric. 2. Visual communications.
    3. Visual perception. 4. Report writing. I. Title.
   PE1408 .H3295 2002
   808'.042—dc21

                         2001038798

9 8 7 6 5 4 3 2 1

First Edition

ISBN 1-57685-405-1

For more information or to place an order, contact LearningExpress at:
900 Broadway
Suite 604
New York, NY 10003

Or visit us at:
  www.learnatest.com

contents

visual **writing**

chapter
one

Organization:

It's Everywhere!

take a look around you. Organization is everywhere. The world is organized as continents, oceans, and atmosphere. Forests are ordered as trees, plants, and animals. Countries take shape as states, cities, counties, and towns. Even your room, whether it's a specific room or merely some space earmarked as yours, has organization, too. In spite of how messy it may be on any given day, your room is organized into the place where you sleep, where you store your CDs, your clothes, and your personal stuff. If you can think of a subject—boys, girls, music, sports, you name it—you can organize it. Why? Because our brains routinely seek out patterns of organization.

the brain's quest to organize saves three astronauts

ONE OF our brain's prime directives, apart from keeping us alive, is to seek meaning out of chaos. This instinctive desire and ability to put things into order is one of humanity's greatest skills. A scene from the movie *Apollo 13* drives the point home.

A flip of a switch yields a spark that triggers a small explosion aboard the Apollo 13 capsule, aborting a trip to the moon for three astronauts. But that's not their only problem. They will soon suffocate from the carbon dioxide their bodies are exhaling. Three astronauts will perish in space unless a solution to their problem is found, fast.

It is at this point that organization saves the day.

A NASA engineer throws ordinary gadgets and widgets onto a conference table around which his NASA colleagues stand. The engineer announces that the pile of what looks like random pieces of junk represents all that the Apollo 13 astronauts have at their disposal on their spacecraft.

Will they be able to build a carbon dioxide filter from this junk? Will they survive? This is the dialogue in the conference room.

. . . the pile of what looks like random pieces of junk represents all that the Apollo 13 astronauts have at their disposal on their spacecraft. Will they survive?

NASA CHIEF ENGINEER:
Okay, people, listen up. The people upstairs handed us this one and we gotta come through. We gotta find a way to make **this** [*a* **box**] *fit into the hole for* **this** (*a* **cylinder**) *using nothing but* **that,** [**the gadgets and widgets** *he's thrown onto the table.*]

ENGINEER₁: *Let's get it organized.*

ENGINEER₂: *Okay, okay: let's build a filter.*

Immediately realizing they must get it organized, they work against the clock to save the three astronauts trapped in a soon-to-be metal gas chamber. After examining and organizing the pile of gadgets and widgets, these skilled engineers ultimately craft a breathing apparatus—a filter, as brilliant as it is crude. The rest of the story is literally history and one of the twentieth century's greatest examples of successful problem solving. How did these engineers do it?

"how to construct a makeshift filter for stranded astronauts"

Do any of us believe that any NASA engineers, who accomplished this formidable task, studied such a topic in any engineering textbook? Of course not! They succeeded because they brainstormed. They successfully analyzed their:

- *subject*—saving astronauts
- *topic or objective*—building a filter that functions as a breathing mechanism
- *supporting details*—using available gadgets and widgets to get the job done

They successfully searched for order and pattern amid clutter and chaos and ultimately synthesized a unique filter that served as the breathing apparatus that saved three lives.

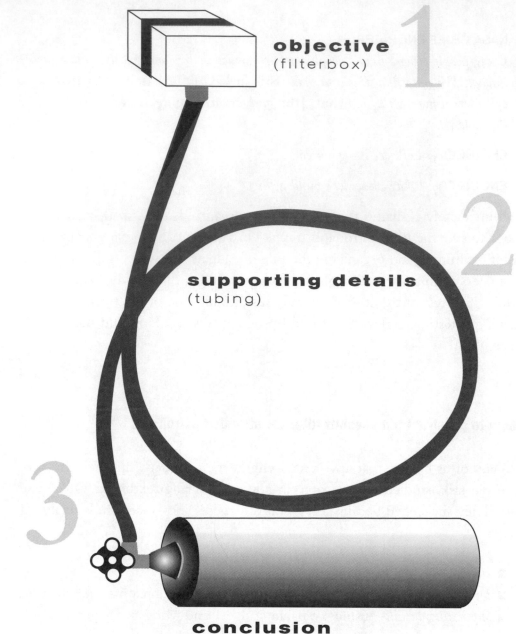

objective
(filterbox)

1

supporting details
(tubing)

2

3

conclusion
(cylinder)

1. The box begins the objective.
2. The middle—the hose—connects the beginning to the end of the objective with supporting details that you organize with graphic organizers.
3. The cylinder, once connected, completes the objective.

how to write an essay
for just about anyone who asks

CONSIDER YOURSELF an astronaut. Not just any astronaut—but an astronaut lost in space—much like the Apollo 13 astronauts. You will potentially suffocate in the capsule chamber of high stakes—*timed* essay tests—that are alien to a writing process that should allow the luxury of time. If it seems like your chamber is getting crammed with more and more demands to write essays, you are not imagining things. Today's teachers not only test the writing skills they teach, but they prepare you for the challenge you are sure to face, if not now, then soon. The state and national standardized essay tests that are part of every student's career assure state and national officials that their education tax dollars are producing competent young writers.

Visual Writing helps weak writers become better writers and strong writers become even stronger, because it teaches them to harness the power of visual maps, the graphic organizers that lead to effective communication. Building stronger communication skills *now* will set you apart from your peers when you enter the job market.

Though it may sound gloomy, there is an upside to all this testing. No matter the origin of essay tests, their topics, or audiences, the more you write and learn how to write, the better you become at writing.

did you know?

Whoever first coined the term *brainstorm* was a genius who knew what he or she was talking about. Scientific brain imaging processes such as MRIs reveal the brain's electronic and chemical thinking processes as different colors. They show that writers who analyze and organize subjects and topics, using word lists and other graphic organizers before writing paragraphs, connect more neural pathways and access more knowledge. During brain-image testing, their writing processes register as energetic bursts of color. There really is a storm brewing in our brains. *Let the fireworks begin!*

make the connection to your writing

TEACHER: Okay, people, listen up. The people upstairs (that would be the state assessment office) handed us this one and we gotta come through.

You gotta find a way to make *your essay's introduction* fit into the hole for *your essay's conclusion*, using nothing but *the details you compile by graphically organizing your word gadgets and widgets*, which you will learn how to do in Chapter Two.

STUDENT₁: *Let's get it organized!*

STUDENT₂: Okay, okay: let's write an essay!

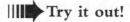 **Try it out!**

"Organization is everywhere." The beginning of this chapter illustrated that the world can be organized as continents, oceans, atmosphere, etc. If you think about it, atoms are organized into molecules. Proteins are organized into cells that are organized into body organs. People are organized into families that are organized into communities that are organized into towns that are organized into counties. Counties are organized into cities that are organized into states that are organized into countries. Now that you have a clearer picture of the many facets of organization, apply your understanding to a warm up exercise.

On the next page, identify organizational components for each of the following: your room, pizza, and zoos. Use the paper on the next page for your response. *(You will find a student example for this on page 8.)*

ORGANIZATIONAL COMPONENTS OF:
My Room, Pizza, and Zoos.

my room:_____

_____

_____

_____

_____

_____

pizza:_____

_____

_____

_____

_____

_____

zoos:_____

_____

_____

_____

_____

_____

ORGANIZATIONAL COMPONENTS OF:
My Room, Pizza, and Zoos.

my room:

bed: sheets, pillows, comforter, bed frame, mattress

carpet, chair, television, dresser, night stand, bed, lamps, standing lamp—all

positioned on the floor

window, shades, curtains, window panes—glass—metal

pizza:

dough, cheese, sauce, oven, chef

"everything" pizza: pepperoni, peppers, olives, onions, sausage, cheese, tomato

sauce, dough

tomato sauce—tomatoes, salt, pepper, spices, heat, spoon, pot, stove to make it

zoos:

cages, animals, trees, trails, houses, staff, food for people and animals

animals: zebras, elephants, alligators, birds, monkeys, lions

habitats: aviary, aquatic, desert, forest, plains, desert

Graphic Organizers:
The Writer's Widgets

okay, we've learned that the essay test is not going away any time soon and that essay tests are not a bad thing because they help us become more effective writers and communicators. But since anxiety is the detour that blocks the road to proficient writing, how will knowing that more writing means better writing help conquer anxiety and writer's block when you face the dreaded essay test? And the higher the test-taking stakes—passing, promotion, graduation—the greater the writing roadblock. Even competent writers in the throes of test anxiety flounder and write essays devoid of organization, and consequently lose out on organizational points. If you haven't already learned how your essays are scored, you need a quick lesson in rubrics.

get the point! know how you'll be scored

RUBRIC IS THE fancy word for *rule*. Rubrics, then, are the rules by which you are scored. There are many variations of rubrics, and largely the form they take depends on the state in which you live. You will learn more about the rules of writing in later chapters. For now, here's a brief look at them:

- *Idea and Content*
- *Organization*
- *Voice*
- *Word Choice*
- *Sentence Fluency*
- *Conventions/Mechanics*

rubrics, word web style

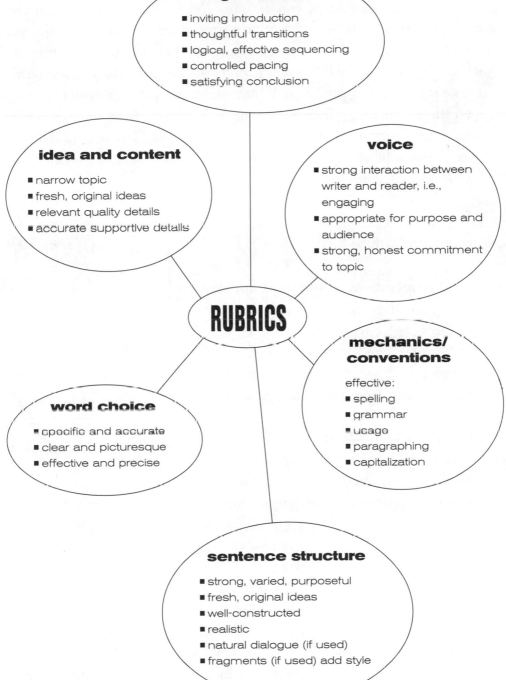

organization
- inviting introduction
- thoughtful transitions
- logical, effective sequencing
- controlled pacing
- satisfying conclusion

idea and content
- narrow topic
- fresh, original ideas
- relevant quality details
- accurate supportive details

voice
- strong interaction between writer and reader, i.e., engaging
- appropriate for purpose and audience
- strong, honest commitment to topic

RUBRICS

mechanics/ conventions
effective:
- spelling
- grammar
- usage
- paragraphing
- capitalization

word choice
- specific and accurate
- clear and picturesque
- effective and precise

sentence structure
- strong, varied, purposeful
- fresh, original ideas
- well-constructed
- realistic
- natural dialogue (if used)
- fragments (if used) add style

The critical minutes you spend organizing your topic through visual writing ensures you an essay with organizational integrity. That organization will help you earn most or all of the points for the *Organization* rubric. But the benefits of visual writing don't stop there. The logical flow established by your essay's visual map helps you see and communicate your central idea more clearly. As a result, you will write a more focused essay that helps you earn more *Content and Idea* points. Visual maps free you from *"Where do I begin?"* and *"How do I end?"* jitters, giving you the freedom and the power to devote more time to your word choice and your sentence structure, earning you the points earmarked for *Writing Style.*

(While visual maps help you with *what* you write, and *how* you mechanically write—your spelling, capitalization, punctuation, etc.—determines the number of *Mechanics/Convention*s points you earn.

the art of visual writing

The word *essay* is derived from the Latin and French words that mean "to attempt" or "trial." How appropriate. An essay is very much like a trial. And you are the defendant! Your writing skills are the defense that determines the verdict. How will you defend yourself? It's up to you.

When you are taking an essay test, you are your sole defense. You are not going to have your teacher or this book around to help you. So you must practice visual writing to learn the art of organization. And *it is an art.*

Visual Writing is designed to help you practice. By reading each chapter and completing each writing activity, you will learn how to write better essays. You will also become a better writer and communicator who knows how to create order out of the seeming clutter and chaos surrounding your ideas, opinions, and knowledge.

An essay is very much like a trial. And you are the defendant! Your writing skills are the defense that determines the verdict. Will you be found guilty or innocent?

essay tests

the nature of the beast called the *essay test*

They're out there. Essay Tests. Waiting to get you if you're not prepared for them. But knowledge is power. The more you know about essay tests, the more you'll be ready for them. There are basically four kinds of writing that spawn those monstrous essay tests. Here's a quick review:

the simple truth about the four kinds of writing

- **Descriptive writing** tests ask you to describe something. Depending on the essay's topic—often called a prompt—you might be asked to describe something or someone real, like a planet or a person. You might have to describe something or someone imaginary, a UFO, or an extraterrestrial.

  The focus of descriptive writing: Effective usage of imagery and sensory details.

- **Narrative writing** tests ask you to tell a story. You might be asked to write the story behind a personal experience, or construct a fictional story using your own imagination with guidance from the prompt.

  The focus of narrative writing: Effective storytelling with attention to characterization, setting, and plot development.

- **Expository writing** tests ask you to inform your reader about a specific topic. Expository essays challenge you to use knowledge you have acquired—via school or life lessons—or there could be certain information included in the test question that you must use as support in your essay.

  The focus of expository writing: Skillful presentation of information on a specific subject or topic.

- **Persuasive writing** tests ask you to persuade your reader to agree with your opinion on a particular subject or topic. Formats required vary from paragraphs to letters, both informal and formal.

  The focus of persuasive writing: Clear, effective argument using logic and reasoning.

writing on demand and braintalks

You might be thinking right about now that writing an essay, no matter what kind, isn't going to be difficult, and you'll be set as long as you read this book and learn how to map your ideas. Unfortunately it's not that simple, because there's one more problem: **TIME!**

Essay tests, especially those high-stakes essay tests that hold everything from passing to promotion in the balance, require that you complete the test in a specific amount of time. That's why you need to *braintalk*. Journals and diaries are good examples of braintalks. A braintalk is simply a talk with your brain on paper. It's like a freewrite directly addressed to one audience: your brain. During an essay test, write a short, fast note to your brain. Explain to it what you have to do and how much time you have. In your braintalk, order your brain to do these things: choose the most effective kind of visual map, construct a visual map that lays out relevant details, and be ready to interpret it so that you can write a great essay.

> When connecting learning styles, you connect neural pathways that activate in your brain. You literally electrify your brain to wake up and get to work!

You might be thinking right about now: "Hey wait a minute! My brain knows what I have to do. It's what helped me read the essay prompt in the first place." True, but brain research supports the wisdom behind using a minute or two to dialogue with yourself, on paper, rather than just thinking.

writing: a whole brain experience

Holding a pen or pencil to paper to write a virtual letter to yourself connects your *kinesthetic* learning style to the *intrapersonal* and *visual* learning styles you've already set in motion by reading and thinking about the essay prompt. The more learning styles★ you connect, the more neural pathways you activate in your brain. You literally electrify your brain to wake up and get to work!

★The brain has many learning styles. To learn more about your brain and how it works, surf the web—keyword: brain. You'll be amazed. Or, go to *brain connections* at www.susd.org/schools/middle/Ingleside/Brain%20Connection%20WebPage/index.htm

Without going into too much detail, the brain has two hemispheres, left and right. While organizing is a predominantly left-brain skill, seeing the big picture behind anything is the job of the right hemisphere. For example, the right side of your brain sees the forest, while the left identifies its components: the trees, leaves, squirrels, acorns, etc. Trust me: A braintalk is the right brain's written request to the left brain for organizational help. Sometimes a few sentences are all you need to ignite the left-brain sparks that help create detailed graphic maps. (See next page for a visual map that explains the concept of the perceptual thinking habits of left and right brains.)

So, are you brain-ready? If you are, *Visual Writing* will show you how to organize your ideas, opinions, and facts so that you can successfully tackle any of today's essays, not to mention tomorrow's far more challenging real life essays—resumes, applications, employee memos, and reports. You get the idea. So let's get started!

part of the brain really can't see the forest for the trees . . .

The right hemisphere of the brain identifies whole pictures. In the case of a forest, it sees the entire forest.

The left hemisphere of the brain identifies the specific components that make up a whole. In the case of a forest: the trees, leaves, squirrels, acorns, etc. The left brain really can't see the forest for the trees!

visual writing challenge #1
create a word web that identifies your room's contents

Think about your room or the space you call home. The examples on the next page will help you get started. Notice how Example 2 is similar to Example 1. Example 2, however, has boxes around groups of words in which titles or headings have been added, "Entertainment Center" and "Magazine Stand." The example illustrates how your left and right brain work together: as the left brainstorms specific details like magazines and books, your right brain helps you define their broader conceptual headings, i.e., "Magazine Stand."

example 1

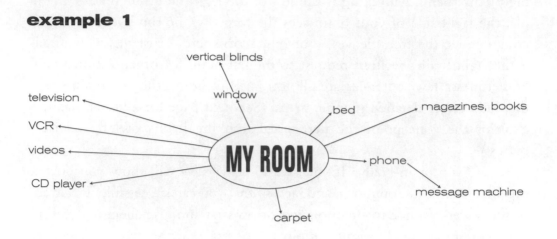

example 2

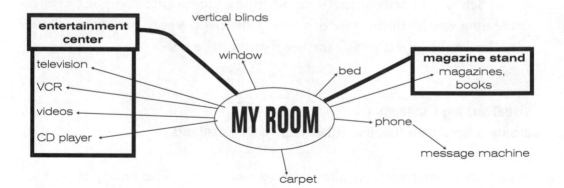

A word web is the perfect graphic organizer for an essay that asks you to describe something. After brainstorming all the details you can, search for patterns or groupings to help you organize further so that you can write a sequentially logical essay.

three

Visual Writing and Cereal

cereal is a popular food whose packaging distinguishes it from all other breakfast foods. Think about it. Have you ever placed an egg carton on the table, so that you could read its information while eating scrambled eggs? Of course not! But cereal boxes, that's another subject. At one time or another, all of us have scanned or read the panels on a cereal box while munching on a crunchy bowl of flakes or puffs. As if browsing through a magazine, we noticed the colorful pictures on the front and back panels, read interesting facts on the informative side panels, enjoyed . . . hey wait!

I've been braintalking! This last sentence is like the braintalk introduced in Chapter Two. It sparked my left brain's desire to graphically organize a word map that depicts the subject of cereal boxes and their characteristics:

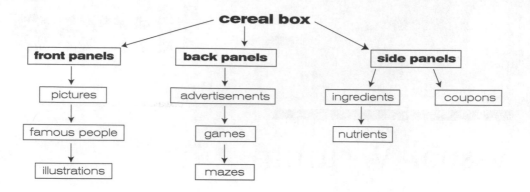

the various kinds of visual writing

In Chapter Two you completed a word web. To get a clearer picture of what visual writing is all about, you need to understand that visual writing comes in many shapes and sizes, and the shapes and sizes you should use depend on what is required by essay topics, also known as essay *prompts*. They are called prompts because they prompt you to think about a topic.

The next section in this chapter presents and explains the variety of visual maps. It includes essay prompts with examples of visual maps constructed for the prompts. Take time to understand each visual map presented, because you'll need them to complete the activities that follow. While the sample visual maps are very different from one another, they all relate to the same subject: cereal.

The samples and activities in this chapter will prepare you for the more complex activities that follow, which ultimately prepare you for the real essay tests that will be thrown onto your desk, much like the gadgets and widgets discussed in Chapter One. *Remember:* NASA engineers faced their problem by working with random miscellany to which they added thought, logic, pattern, discovery, and solution. Consider yourself a writing engineer who uses visual maps to graphically organize solutions for every essay challenge whether descriptive, narrative, informative, or persuasive. The types you'll use most often are:

- Venn Diagrams
- Hierarchical Maps
- Sequential Charts
- Cyclical Maps
- Word Webs
- Plot Diagrams

NASA engineers faced their challenge by working with random miscellany to which they added thought, logic, pattern, discovery, and solution. Consider yourself a writing engineer . . .

the Venn diagram

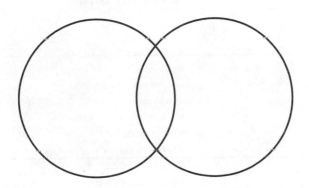

The **Venn diagram** is a conceptual map consisting of two overlapping circles that create three sections.

By writing words and phrases into the appropriate section, writers *see* the similarities and differences between an essay's stated topics.

The Venn diagram is very useful when you are asked to compare and contrast two concepts, two people, or different customs.

Essay prompts signal the usefulness of Venn diagrams when they include phrases like:

- compare and contrast
- choose between
- distinguish between
- decide between

Venn diagram

Cereal Essay Prompt #1: **You are asked to decide the menu for your club's end-of-year breakfast meeting: cereal or bacon and eggs? Convince your fellow members that your choice of breakfast is the best choice. (Persuasion)**

A Venn diagram becomes very useful when asked to distinguish between two of anything! Its overlapping circles help you to *see* similarities and differences.

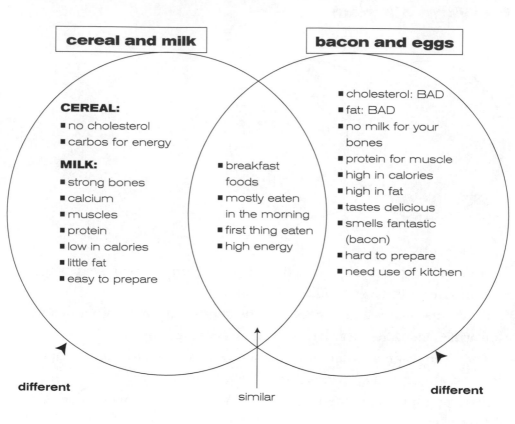

cereal and milk

bacon and eggs

CEREAL:
- no cholesterol
- carbos for energy

MILK:
- strong bones
- calcium
- muscles
- protein
- low in calories
- little fat
- easy to prepare

- breakfast foods
- mostly eaten in the morning
- first thing eaten
- high energy

- cholesterol: BAD
- fat: BAD
- no milk for your bones
- protein for muscle
- high in calories
- high in fat
- tastes delicious
- smells fantastic (bacon)
- hard to prepare
- need use of kitchen

different   similar   **different**

Depending on your knowledge base, you might add specific vitamins and minerals to the Venn diagram shown. Whatever you add, it is pretty clear that there is very little similarity. The choice is now up to you. Do you argue in favor of the healthy and easily prepared cereal breakfast? Or do you persuade your reader that the aromatic, delicious bacon and egg breakfast is worth the added difficulty of its preparation? Whatever you decide, the Venn diagram organized your ideas. It has also set a stage to showcase your writer's *voice*, when you write your essay. (More about the rubric called *Voice* in Chapter Five.)

> **Breakfast cereal will keep us all heart healthy and help us win the battle of the bulge!**
>
> **Who wants to settle for a soggy bowl of cereal when you can enjoy delectably fried eggs served with delicious-tasting, crisply fried bacon? Come on. You only live once.**
>
> **The Venn diagram has set a stage to showcase your writer's voice when you write your essay.**

hierarchical map

A **hierarchical map** is a conceptual map that deals with main concepts and subconcepts.

A hierarchical map starts with a shape—for example, a rectangle—in which a main concept or category is written. Analysis of the concepts produces subconcepts, subcategories, sublevels, etc. The word widgets for these subconcepts are written within shapes comparable to and beneath the main concept, establishing the hierarchy or pecking order.

Essay prompts signal the usefulness of *hierarchical maps* when they include words like:

- analyze
- classify
- divide
- categorize

hierarchical map

Cereal Essay Prompt #2: **You are given random cereal boxes. Using information gathered from the boxes, identify the nutritional benefits derived from eating cereal for breakfast. (Informative)**

A *hierarchical map* suits this essay. You start with a main *concept*, like "Cereal Breakfast Nutrition," and chart *subconcepts* beneath it as they are identified, i.e., milk and corn flakes, vitamins, protein, etc.

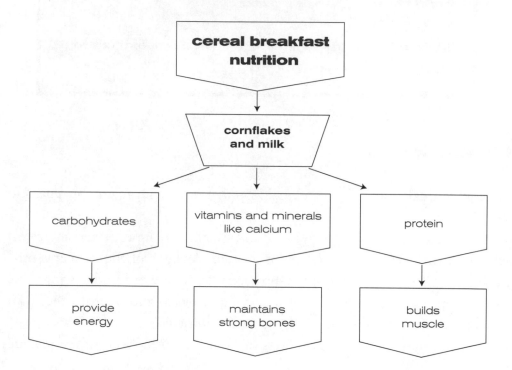

sequential chart

A **sequential chart** is a conceptual map that charts the sequence of specific events using a linear (resembling a straight line) pattern of organization. Charting events on a timeline is the perfect example of a sequential chart.

Essays will sometimes ask you to write about the cause and effect of a particular event, a battle for example. When they do, sequential charts are the maps to use.

Essay prompts signal the usefulness of *sequential charts* when they include words like:

- show, describe, *or* explain the . . .
- cause and effect
- chronological order
- sequence
- events

sequential chart

Cereal Essay Prompt #3: **Describe what happens to a bowl of cereal that sits too long. (Description)**

A **sequential chart** is perfect for this essay because it clearly asks the writer to describe a sequence of events. Here are two versions of a sequential chart to show you that you can add your brain's artistic personality to your sequential charts.

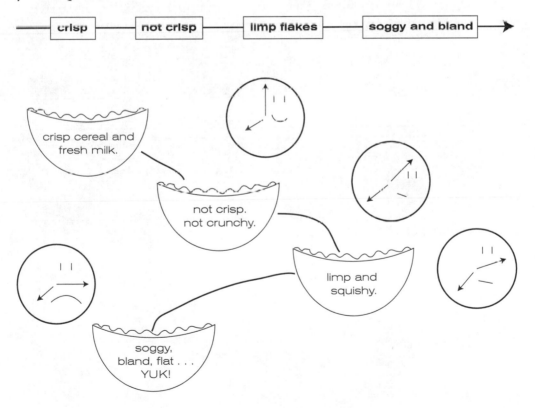

cyclical map

A **cyclical map** is constructed using a circle or cyclical shape. It is most useful to represent events that are part of a continuous cycle, for example, day turns to night, which turns into day, etc.

Any time an essay directs you to write about a topic that involves a continuous process or sequence, you should create a cyclical map, which illustrates the continuous or cyclical nature of that process.

Circular or clock-like by design, cyclical maps help you recall the details, whether sequentially, hourly, seasonally, etc.

Essay prompts signal the usefulness of *cyclical maps* when they include words like:

- continuous
- cyclical
- process of
- life of

make the connection to your writing

TRY IT OUT!

Cereal Essay Prompt #4: **Use prose or poetry to describe a typical day in the life of a teenager. Just account for your routine. (Description/Informative)★**

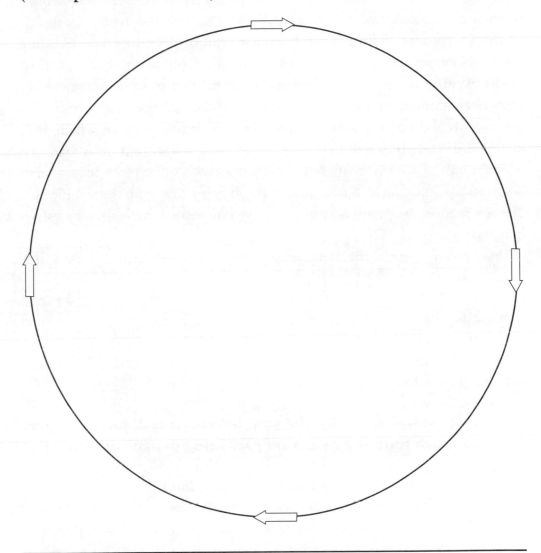

★This essay prompt provides you the freedom to choose between two kinds of writing: *informative* paragraphs or *descriptive* writing, i.e., poetry which will produce the (sensory) images found in your typical day, rather than describe or explain them more formally.

The *cyclical map* and its characteristic circle help you recall more details in your typical twenty-four hour day.

word web

A **word web** is a group of words or word phrases that graphically connect back to and branch out from a central concept. The words in a word web are often encircled and then connected with lines back to the main concept.

Word webs lend themselves to the freest kind of brainstorming. Creating them is like playing a game of word association on paper. Each word or phrase written on a paper can trigger another. The topic requirements of each essay prompt determine your web's words and phrases. And sometimes your words and phrases become mini-concepts or subconcepts, which generate words and phrases that connect back to and branch out from them.

Interpreting word webs is essential when essays require more than a mere description. Studying a completed word web helps you grasp the significance of each section, helping you make the big connection back to your essay's demands.

Essay prompts signal the usefulness of *word webs* when they include words like:

- create
- connect
- solve
- interpret why

Cereal Essay Prompt #5: **Why do you believe cereal manufacturers spend so much time and money on packaging design? (Informative)**

A *word web* helps you recall details—in this case, from all those cereal boxes you've stared at over the years. But notice that this essay asks you to *analyze* your gathered information. Here's where the value of a quick braintalk enters. A fast note to yourself before organizing fires up your neural pathways to find clues to the answer. A follow-up braintalk that asks the brain to *interpret* data produces the answer; more about follow-up braintalks on page 30.

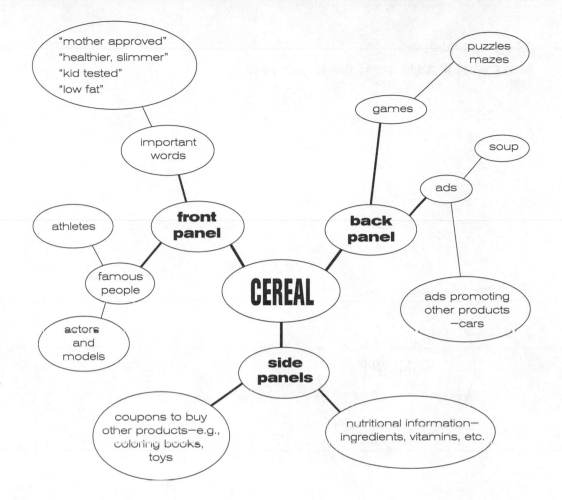

By the way, if you're wondering why a word web is used here, when a similar task done in Chapter Two used a hierarchical chart, repeat after me: *There is usually more than one way to solve a problem!*

Essay #5
WORD WEB

Okay. My left brain
did a great word web, separating
all the parts of a cereal box. Now, Brain, let's make the connections!
What's my word web telling me? Hmmm. Let's take a serious look: The colors
are attractive . . . the games are cool . . . so are the people they put on the boxes.
But some of these words just don't have anything to do with cereal. I'll <u>underline</u>
them: <u>famous people</u>, <u>ads selling cars</u> and <u>soup</u>—nothing to do with eating cereal.
Hey, that's it! They're using the boxes for <u>advertising</u>. The colors, games, and
people . . . that's how they grab my attention. But selling me something
else . . . that's what they're really trying to do! . . . Hey, follow-up
braintalking really works! And Chapter Four's 1-2-3 Maps will show me
how to put it all together!

plot diagram

A **plot diagram** is a graphic rendering of the main events of a factual or fictional story. One diagonal line represents the rising action of a story. A shorter line to the right represents the falling action, resolution, or to put it simply: what happens at the end. A dot connects the two lines, representing the high point of a story, or climax, after which everything falls into place.

Plot diagrams help writers write about a personal experience or create a fictional story that is based on specific directions. With important minutes ticking away from the finite amount of time essay tests allow, a plot diagram helps you quickly map out a sequence of events that suits your essay's directive and helps maintain the focus of your story. Because stories—whether real or imaginary—include settings and characters, plot diagrams should really be one part of a story map, which includes two important word webs: one for setting and one (at least) for the main character.

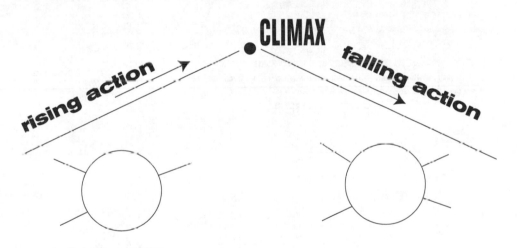

Essay prompts signal the usefulness of plot diagrams and story maps when they include the phrases (no surprise here):

- Write a story . . .
- Share an experience, real or imaginary . . .

plot diagram

Cereal Essay Prompt #6: **Write a story about a girl who breaks her tooth on the prize inside a cereal box. (Narration)**

A *plot diagram* is important to the writer asked to write a story, because it allows you to map out a sequence of events that suits the essay's directive and helps maintain your story's focus. Don't forget quick word webs to establish your setting and characters. Of course, a braintalk like the one to the right will help too!

Braintalk: *Okay, Brain, you have 30 minutes. Figure out where, who, and how. She breaks a tooth . . . so what? Make it funny . . . How? Make her a brat!*

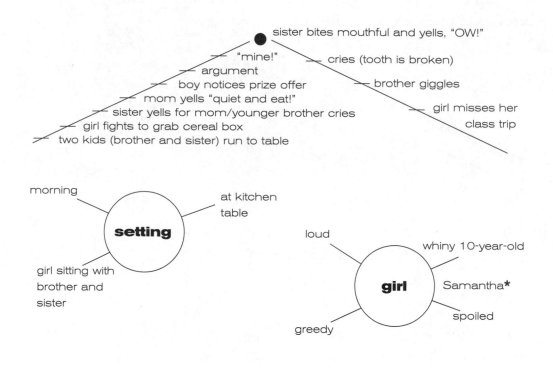

---

*The name of the main character, Samantha, came to mind only after writing on the plot diagram that mom yells for quiet. Don't waste time thinking of names for characters. Their names emerge as you develop your story and your characters come alive.

The visual maps based on prompts regarding cereal (including the cyclical map you created for your typical day), have prepared you for the next set of activities. Suggestions will be offered, but you decide which visual map best suits each prompt. **Remember: Your visual maps are graphic organizers that lead to bigger and better things to follow: 1-2-3 maps and essays!**

You are on your way to discovering how visual maps are the graphic organizers that fit into 1-2-3 maps that produce effective essays.

Right now—practice with pizza!

TRY IT OUT:

- **Descriptive:** *Describe the condition of a pepperoni pizza that has been delivered—one hour late!*
- **Narrative:** *Write a story about a teenage boy who ate a whole pizza.*
- **Informative:** *Use any resources available to you (including Web or textual searches) to write a speech that explains why pizza provides a nutritionally sound meal.*
- **Persuasive:** *Your science teacher has asked the class to determine which meal contains more nutritional value: two slices of pizza OR turkey on whole wheat. Using what you know about these foods, convince your teacher that your answer is correct.*

hint:

PIZZA ACTIVITY #2 NARRATIVE:

Write a story about a teenage boy who ate a whole pizza.

hint:

PIZZA ACTIVITY #3 INFORMATIVE:

Use any resources available to you
(including the Web or books) to write a speech that
explains why pizza provides a nutritionally sound meal.

hint:

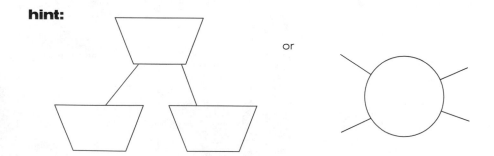

or

PIZZA ACTIVITY #4 PERSUASIVE:

Your science teacher has asked the class to determine which meal contains more nutritional value—two slices of pizza, or turkey on whole wheat. Using what you know about these foods, convince your teacher that your answer is correct.

hint:

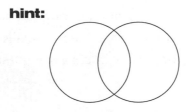

make the connection to your writing

sharpening your organizational skills

Before continuing your exploration of *Visual Writing*, complete the activities below to reinforce your understanding of the value of visual writing. The more you practice graphic organizing in a non–threatening environment—wherever you are right now—the more you will be able to comfortably and confidently call upon your skills when your environment is a little more threatening: the essay testing room!

1. Create a visual map that graphically organizes all aspects of a zoo.

2. Think about the following essay topics, each of them concerning zoos:
   a. Describe the day in the life of a particular animal living at the zoo.
   b. Share your fondest or worst experience related to a visit to the zoo.
   c. Prepare a speech for your school's foreign exchange students who will be touring your local zoo. Use what you know about your local zoo or zoos in general to explain to them what they can expect from their visit.
   d. Many people believe that zoos provide a wonderful opportunity to see and experience animals they would otherwise never see. Animal rights activists contend that zoos are inhumane. Write an essay that expresses your viewpoint.

3. Now that you have read each of the topics above, consider the following:
   a. Is my map about zoos thorough enough to answer one or more of the prompts above or are there more details I must add so that I might respond to, or *address*, these essay questions?

    b. Are some details relevant to one essay prompt but not the others?

    c. What other graphic organizers might I construct that would be more useful to addressing particular prompts? (Example: a plot diagram for Essay B.)

4. Define or explain each of the graphic organizers listed below and the types of essays for which they are best suited. (You may want to construct a visual map to answer this question . . . Hint, hint.) You can write your answers on page 40.

    ■ Hierarchical map
    ■ Venn Diagram
    ■ Sequential Chart
    ■ Cyclical Map
    ■ Word Web
    ■ Plot Diagram

5. What is the purpose of a follow-up braintalk? You can write your answers on page 40.

When you finish this section, you'll be ready to learn about 1–2–3 maps!

four

1-2-3 Maps:
Using Visual Maps
to Write Essays

by now you understand visual maps, the many varieties you can create, and their usefulness during those nail-biting, heart-stopping moments when you must face essay tests.

But how does a visual map translate into *prose* on the essay, the fancy word for ordinary writing otherwise known as sentences and paragraphs? How do you transform Venn or plot diagrams, word maps, etc., into the introductory, body, and concluding paragraphs required of essays? It's as easy as one, two, three.

putting it all together

In Chapter Three you constructed a variety of visual maps based on essay prompts all related to cereal, so you should have proven to yourself that you and your brain really know how to pick things apart. If so, you are ready to learn how your already-prepared visual maps become the middle sections of 1-2-3 maps.

1-2-3 maps organize your 1) introductory, 2) body, and 3) concluding paragraphs. Whether you write one or one hundred paragraphs, an essay *must* have an introduction, a body of supporting details, and a conclusion.

The 1-2-3 map graphically separates each of these important sections, reminding you of their order.

Let's consider the filtering system that saved the Apollo 13 astronauts again, only now we will relate it to the 1-2-3 map. The objective of the Apollo 13 engineers was to build a filtering system that would ensure safe air for the endangered astronauts. The engineers meeting their objective depended on three sections: a box, a cylinder, and a hose in the middle that would ultimately connect them. Though the parts were very distinct, their connection was critical to the success of that objective. Each essay you write has an objective, too. Determined by your essay prompt, that objective relies on three sections: an introduction, a conclusion, and a body of support in the middle that ultimately connects them. Like the air filter parts, the connection of the three sections is very critical to the quality, and therefore success, of your essay.

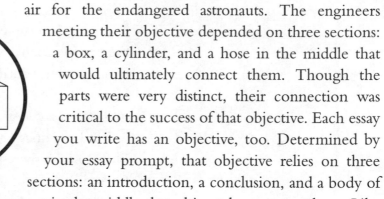

The first and last shapes of your 1-2-3 map compare to the Apollo 13 box and cylinder, and the middle part, your graphic organizer, is word widgets and gadgets that connect those parts!

1-2-3 maps—breathing life into your essays

Let's use the Venn diagram constructed in Chapter Three, which contrasted the differences between cereal and bacon and eggs for breakfast. Sure, the Venn diagram clearly separated the information necessary to respond to the essay prompt that asked the writer to choose between breakfasts, but now what? Where do you begin? And *begin* is what you must do to write an essay!

the 1-2-3 plan

NO MATTER HOW many pages you take to write an essay, each page and each paragraph is connected to the other. The connecting sections can be summed up in several different sets of three words: beginning, middle, end; start, middle, finish; introduction, body, conclusion: 1-2-3.

So, where do you find the *first* part of your essay in Venn or plot diagrams, or cyclical maps? You don't—not unless you construct and complete the graphic organizer appropriate for each essay, as part of a 1-2-3 map. The 1-2-3 map borrows shapes used by the Apollo 13 engineers for their air filter solution. The box and cylinder fit our 1-2-3 map objective perfectly.

constructing a 1-2-3 map for an essay

1. At the top of your paper, draw a small box and write key words that identify the essay's objective, topic, purpose, etc.
2. At the bottom, draw a small cylinder in which you write the same words that were written in the box.
3. In the middle, construct and complete the graphic organizer appropriate to the essay objective, then draw a circle (the hose!) around it, connecting your middle to the top and bottom.

There you have it! The organization for your opening, middle, and closing paragraphs. Let's take a look at how a 1-2-3 Map connects all the parts of a well-constructed essay.

a visual on the 1-2-3 map

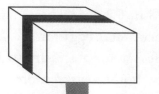

1

write your essay's objective here in your opening.

2

construct the graphic organizer that best suits your essay prompt in this space. The connecting hose encircles the supporting details that your visual map generates. The hose encircling these details reminds you to connect your graphic organizer with opening and closing paragraphs, which identify your essay's objective.

3

write your objective here too, so you remember to restate it in your conclusion.

follow-up braintalks

After setting up your 1-2-3 map, you will want to conduct a follow-up braintalk, mentioned in Chapter Three. Whether mental or written, the follow-up directs your brain to sequence or reorganize your middle map's words and phrases so that you can effectively apply your 1-2-3 map's contents to well-written paragraphs.

Follow-Up Braintalk: *I need to work on my middle map so my essay runs smoothly—from start to finish!*

---

the 1-2-3 map and follow-up braintalk

cereal essay # 1

YOU WILL NOTICE a few additions to the original map in Chapter Three, which compared cereal to bacon and egg breakfasts: the box and cylinder. You see the objective of the essay twice, once in the box and once again in the cylinder shape, reminding the writer that effective essays always state and restate an essay's purpose in both the introductory and concluding paragraphs.

> The hose is drawn to remind you that the middle part, which becomes the body paragraphs, must connect your beginning to your ending. The more you practice the 1-2-3 Map, the subtler your connectors can be.

The shapes, borrowed from the Apollo 13 shapes, are connected to one another by, in this case, a Venn diagram. The diagram contains the details that distinguish the two breakfasts. The hose is drawn to remind you that the middle part, which becomes the body paragraphs, must connect your beginning to your ending. The more you practice the 1-2-3 map, the less need you have to actually draw the connectors.

As you examine this 1-2-3 map, read the follow-up braintalk carefully and pay attention to the additions that were made to the original Venn diagram. You will read the essay generated by the map shortly.

making connections to your writing

How is the box like an introductory paragraph?
How is the visual map encircled by a hose like body paragraphs?
How is the cylinder like a concluding paragraph?

You will find the answers to the questions in this chapter. Now let's have a look at the essays about cereal. When you notice that the 1-2-3 map designs and shapes differ, remember: artistic creativity is permissible!

---

venn diagram 1-2-3 map

Recall: *Cereal Essay #1:* **You are asked to choose your club's end-of-year breakfast meeting menu: cereal or bacon and eggs? Convince your fellow members that your choice of breakfast is the best choice.**

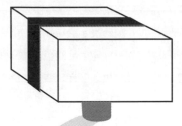

best choice: cereal.
**bacon and eggs taste good
but they're bad for you.**

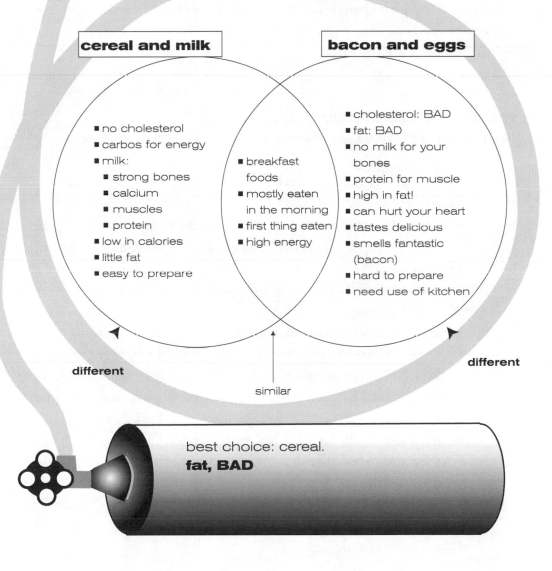

cereal and milk

- no cholesterol
- carbos for energy
- milk:
  - strong bones
  - calcium
  - muscles
  - protein
- low in calories
- little fat
- easy to prepare

- breakfast
  foods
- mostly eaten
  in the morning
- first thing eaten
- high energy

bacon and eggs

- cholesterol: BAD
- fat: BAD
- no milk for your
  bones
- protein for muscle
- high in fat!
- can hurt your heart
- tastes delicious
- smells fantastic
  (bacon)
- hard to prepare
- need use of kitchen

different

different

similar

best choice: cereal.
fat, BAD

Follow-up Braintalk: *Okay, I think cereal is the best choice, so I put that in my opening and closing. I wrote a lot of facts in my Venn diagram. Now what? My opening should grab attention. I'll <u>open</u> with the "<u>fat</u>" and "<u>bad</u>" stuff. I'll put all the good stuff about cereal in the <u>middle</u> and I'll <u>end</u> with how bacon and eggs might smell and <u>taste</u> <u>good</u>, <u>but</u> <u>they're</u> bad for you. Being breakfast foods is the only thing they have in common. I'll use that in my opening and closing.*

from 1-2-3 maps to essays

Cereal Essay Prompt #1: **You are asked to decide the menu for your club's end-of-year breakfast meeting: cereal or bacon and eggs? Convince your fellow members that your choice of breakfast is the best choice. (Persuasion)**

venn diagram student sample
(Notice how the concepts in the Venn diagram on the previous page appear in the essay.)

Cholesterol. Fat. Two bad, bad, words in our health-conscious society. How can anyone think that a bacon and eggs breakfast would be the choice to make for our club's last meeting? Sure, everyone needs the energy they get from breakfast, and bacon and eggs is a breakfast meal. But is it a good one? NO! Cereal, on the other hand, is a good meal and my choice for our end-of-year breakfast meeting.

First of all, you always pour milk on cereal so that means calcium. And calcium means strong bones. And if you're wondering, 2% fat milk has just as much calcium as whole milk with hardly any fat so we should use 2%. If strong bones are important to you then so are muscles, especially if you want to look buff. Since milk is a protein food it will be good for your muscles.

As for the cereal part of a cereal and milk breakfast, it is usually no fat or low fat. Sure, cereal will keep you thin, but that's not the reason we should serve it at our breakfast. The real reason is carbohydrates, which give us energy—energy to keep up with school, sports, and more.

I agree with my fellow club members who may say that bacon and eggs smell so good and taste so good, but eat enough of them and they will make you fat and clog your arteries. And did anyone here think of who's going to cook them? And where? Our club members have worked hard this year. We shouldn't do more work now! Cereal is so easy: milk, box, and bowl. Eat.

I think I proved my point. The only thing these breakfast foods have in common is the fact that they are breakfast foods. Though bacon and eggs wins the taste contest for some, I say let's go with the healthier cereal breakfast. Now . . . when do we eat?

hierarchical 1-2-3

Map Recall: *Cereal Essay #2:* **Using information gathered from random cereal boxes given to you, identify the nutritional benefits derived from eating a cereal breakfast. (Informative)**

Braintalk: Just follow the flow. It's very clear. Summarize the three benefits in the end.

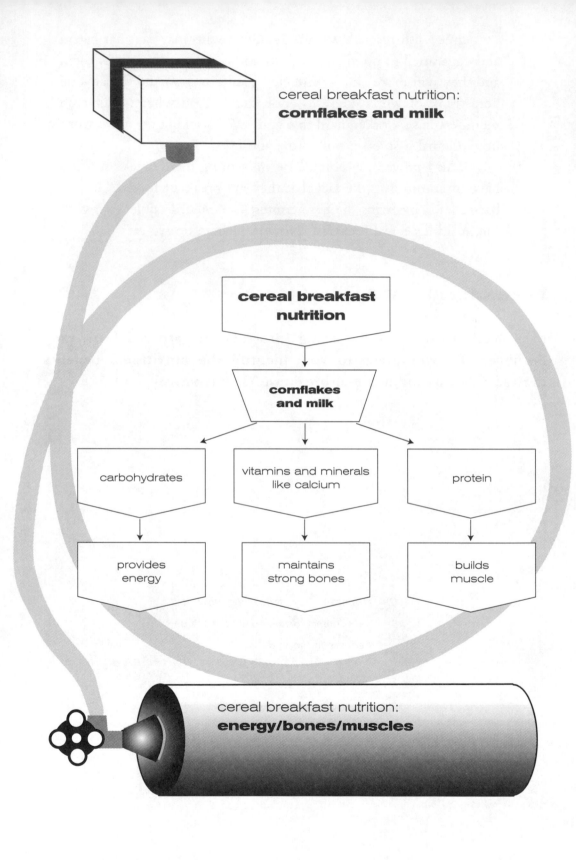

cereal breakfast nutrition:
cornflakes and milk

cereal breakfast nutrition

cornflakes and milk

carbohydrates

vitamins and minerals like calcium

protein

provides energy

maintains strong bones

builds muscle

cereal breakfast nutrition:
energy/bones/muscles

hierarchical student sample 1:

So how many paragraphs will this essay have? From the looks of the 1-2-3 map, there will be three. If the writer plans to develop each subconcept, it may contain five. Let's see how one student did it.

the breakfast of champions

How do you choose your breakfast foods? Do you like convenience—do you choose a Pop-Tart® kind of food? Or do you want nutrition and therefore choose a breakfast cereal? That's what I do, and I do it for three reasons: carbohydrates, vitamins and minerals, and protein.

Cereal is a major source of carbohydrates. By the time you reach junior high school, you know that carbohydrates provide the body with the energy it needs to function. Our bodies do not do anything without carbohydrates. Thinking, running, writing, and everything else the body does needs energy, and cereal provides it.

If you take a look at the side of any cereal box, you will see a breakdown of its vitamins and minerals. There are a lot of them too, and they are all good for your body. But the best thing a cereal breakfast contains is calcium. That's because of the milk you add to your cereal. You don't eat it dry, do you? How often have you been reminded by your parents to drink your milk? It's good for your bones. Well, they're right. As teenagers we need to remember our bones; they're still growing. If we don't supply them with foods like milk, then we risk breaking our bones and not developing them properly. Most teenagers drink Coke, Pepsi, or Gatorade during the day, so it just makes sense to eat a breakfast cereal, *and* add milk to that cereal so we get our calcium.

Besides calcium, milk is also a good protein source. The cereal has a little protein too, but the milk has more. Protein is an essential nutrient that maintains, repairs, and builds our muscles. It's even good for our blood somehow.

By now you know about the nutritional benefits that a cereal breakfast supplies. It will start your day off right with a blast of energy. Cereal gives you strong bones because when you eat it with milk you get calcium, in addition to all the vitamins and minerals that the cereal and milk have for your body. And finally, a cereal breakfast helps your muscles stay fit because of its protein. There you have it. Cereal really is the "breakfast of champions."

Sample 1 did have five paragraphs. Did you know that she added that great title "Breakfast of Champions," after she wrote her last sentence? That's how she got the idea for it. Now let's have a look at Sample 2, a shorter essay using the same visual map. It won't be as developed as the five-paragraph essay above, but maybe it will still be good.

hierarchical student sample 2:

cereal

Cereal is a very nutritious food. When you add milk, it's an excellent source of many nutrients. I will discuss the nutrients in a corn flakes and milk breakfast. They are carbohydrates, vitamins and minerals, and protein.

Milk provides protein, which builds our muscles. Cereal has some protein but not as much as milk. Carbohydrates are important because they give our bodies energy. Vitamins and minerals are important because they maintain all our bodies' functions. Calcium, which is a mineral found in milk, is very important for strong bones.

This essay doesn't make sense and it's boring. The information may be right but it's all mixed up. And it's flat.

This writer needs to remember to use the 1–2–3 map and *voice*, the writer's tool that prevents flat writing. Chapter Five describes strategies that add voice to writing; it's like pulling the audience in with questions as in Sample 1.

word web's 1-2-3 map

Recall: *Cereal Essay #5:* **Why do you believe cereal manufacturers spend so much time and money on packaging design? (Informative)**

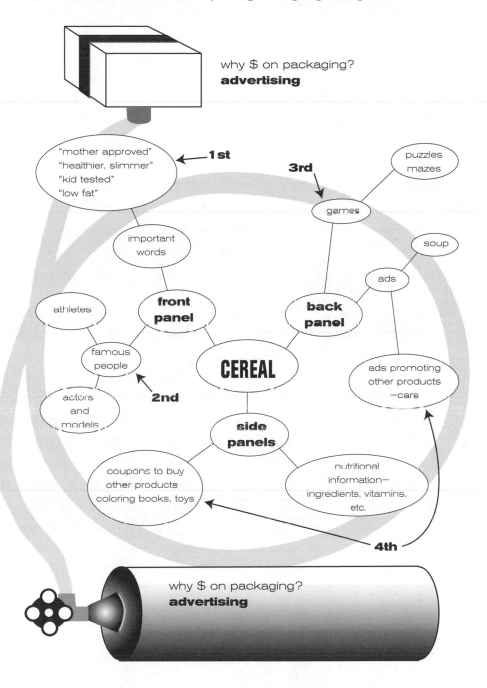

why $ on packaging?
advertising

"mother approved"
"healthier, slimmer"
"kid tested"
"low fat"

1st

3rd

puzzles
mazes

games

important
words

soup

ads

athletes

**front
panel**

**back
panel**

famous
people

CEREAL

ads promoting
other products
—cars

actors
and
models

2nd

**side
panels**

coupons to buy
other products
coloring books, toys

nutritional
information—
ingredients, vitamins,
etc.

4th

why $ on packaging?
advertising

word web student sample

This student wrote: "Important words—people—games—ads" on top of her paper to remind herself of the main ideas she had identified in her word map. Notice how each of those words guide her body paragraphs.

Important words—people—games—ads

catching the consumer

"Mother approved." Anyone would eat a cereal that had "mother approved" stamped on the front of the box. "Kid tested." Kids would eat that cereal, wouldn't they? These are two phrases I saw while I was examining cereal boxes. But the question is why do cereal manufacturers spend so much money on packaging their product? After a closer look at many cereal boxes, I have come up with the answer. And it has nothing to do with kids testing or mothers approving anything. It has to do with advertising.

If you think about it, it makes sense. They spend loads of money—probably millions—to get famous athletes like Michael Jordan to pose for the front of cereal boxes. Why would they spend so much money unless they were going to make more money? To understand how they make more money, you need to look at all the panels of a cereal box carefully.

On the back you will usually see fun games like crossword puzzles and mazes. But you will also see advertisements. I had one box of cereal that was advertising pickup trucks and another that was advertising soup. Soup! After I saw that, I looked to the side panels and saw ingredients and nutrition charts, but I also saw coupons too.

Cereal boxes have all kinds of coupons. Some coupons let you buy products, while others allow you to get information about different products. One box had a coupon for a Sesame Street coloring book. What little kid wouldn't ask for that? Of course, their parents will probably buy it, and they don't even have to go to the store to buy it.

So why do cereal manufacturers spend so much time and money on packaging? Because those bright boxes give them a chance for advertising. General Mills, Post, and Kellogg's spend a lot of time learning about consumers, and they learned that the cereal box packaging will help them catch the consumers who read those boxes and buy the products they advertise.

sequential chart 1-2-3 map

Recall: *Cereal Essay #3:* **Describe what happens to a bowl of cereal that sits too long. (Description)**

Some 1-2-3 maps are really easy! The box and cylinder will remind this writer to open and close his essay properly. He wrote the same thing in both shapes and added "Terrible!" to the closing. That proves he probably understands the rules for "organization." He knows that the ending must be like the opening but a little different, so that readers will finish reading the essay feeling satisfied. Let's see if he succeeds.

sequential chart student sample

time: cereal's enemy

Cereal is usually a delicious, crunchy treat. But when you leave it in your bowl too long, a few things will happen and none of them are good. Let's say you pour milk on your cereal and then leave the table to get something. Even if it's just for a few minutes the cereal will lose its crunch. It will look a little paler too, but your milk will probably have new color. If it's a cereal like Fruit Loops, then the milk will be light pink. A little longer and really bad things start happening. Take a bite. The cereal is limp. There's nothing to chew. Your tongue can just mash it! The more time cereal lays in the bowl, the worse it gets—then it's totally soggy and bland. You'll probably grab a frozen waffle and eat that before you would want to eat an old bowl of mushy cereal. Terrible! There's a saying that time waits for no man. It doesn't wait for cereal either.

That's a great title and a pretty clever ending that suits it. But . . . they're not in the 1-2-3 Map. Where did they come from?

The organization derived from 1-2-3 maps provides writers with more time to work on their word choice and sentence structure!

plot diagram 1-2-3

Map Recall: *Cereal Essay #6:* **Write a story about a girl who breaks her tooth on the prize inside a cereal box. (Narration: refer back to Chapter Three to review the need for setting and character word webs.)**

Braintalk: Okay, Brain, you have 50 minutes. Figure out where, who, and how. She breaks a tooth . . . so what? Make it funny . . How? Make her a brat!

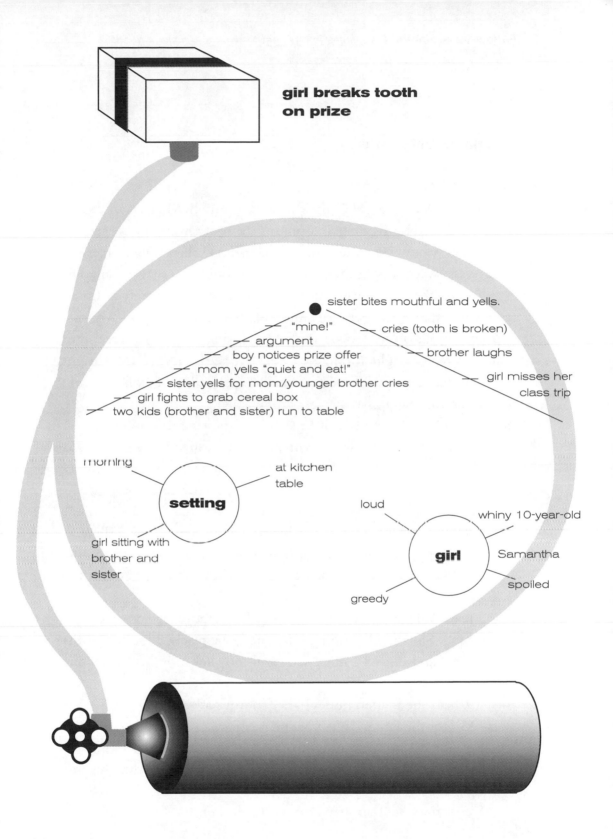

girl breaks tooth on prize

sister bites mouthful and yells.

"mine!" cries (tooth is broken)

argument brother laughs

boy notices prize offer

mom yells "quiet and eat!" girl misses her class trip

sister yells for mom/younger brother cries

girl fights to grab cereal box

two kids (brother and sister) run to table

morning at kitchen table

setting

girl sitting with brother and sister

loud whiny 10-year-old

girl Samantha

greedy spoiled

plot diagram student sample

the stupid magic ring

"Breakfast's on the table!" their mother shouted. Michael and Katie ran to the table, giggling and poking each other as they went.

"Will you two brats keep quiet," Samantha yelled. Their older sister was always bossing them around. Although the twins wanted to yell back, they didn't dare. Samantha could get really nasty at times.

Samantha sat in her seat and watched impatiently as Michael poured milk on his Cocoa Puffs and Katie poured the cereal into her bowl. Bright orange letters "FREE INSIDE" caught Samantha's attention. She immediately grabbed the box from Katie who cried, "Hey, give that back!"

"No way, brat. Not until I get the magic ring. It's mine!"

"Mom," Michael yelled, "Samantha won't give Katie the Cocoa Puffs!"

"MOM!" Katie screamed, "I was pouring my cereal and . . . "

"Both of you . . . quiet!" their mother yelled.

Samantha smirked since she knew her mother wasn't yelling at her. Her brother and sister frowned and pushed away from the table. They ran to get their mother who was walking towards the kitchen.

Meanwhile, Samantha was forcing her hand deep into the box. Nothing. She found nothing. Disgusted, she reached for her brother's bowl and shoved a huge spoonful into her mouth. "OW!" she howled.

"What's the matter, honey?" her mother asked.

"My tooth, agh . . . it's broken!"

Samantha's mother rushed to her side. Samantha was right. She was holding a part of her tooth in her hand along with the free magic ring she had been searching for.

Samantha's mother tried to comfort her but it was no use.

Samantha was bawling. Her mother picked up the phone and told her daughter she would get her into the dentist's office immediately. Now the twins giggled and made faces at their big sister, but Samantha was too upset to mind them. She was now thinking about the field trip to the city that she would miss, all because of that stupid prize in the cereal box.

make the connection to your writing

student sample essay "my room"

Reconsider the word web from Chapter Two entitled "My Room." You will notice that for this sample the introductory and concluding shapes have been added by the writer to complete his 1-2-3 map. Examine his essay's prompt and essay, which follow.

essay prompt

Your cousin is visiting from out of town and will be staying with you for a week. Write an essay that describes your room so that your cousin will know what to expect.

1-2-3 map and braintalk: my room

Braintalk: *My <u>cousin</u> needs to know about my <u>room</u> before he comes. No problem. Entertainment first. The fact that it's a cool room last.*

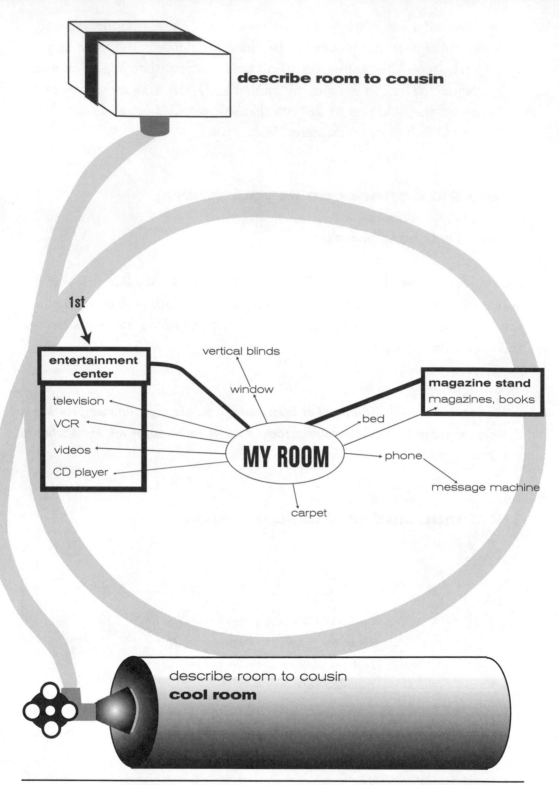

describe room to cousin

1st

entertainment
center

- television
- VCR
- videos
- CD player

vertical blinds

window

MY ROOM

bed

phone

message machine

carpet

magazine stand
magazines, books

describe room to cousin
cool room

This student did not conduct a follow-up braintalk. He felt he was clear as to what he had to do for this essay. His braintalk was a *mental* rather than *written* conversation and is recreated to represent its content.

Hey Jeff,

How's it going? Before you come over I thought I'd let you know about where you'll be staying. You haven't been here in a while. I finally have my own room. It's small, but it's pretty cool. Bring any CDs you like because I have my own TV and stereo. They're built into my entertainment center. There's room for a computer on it, but so far that space is empty. I'm still trying to talk my parents into getting me one for my room. In the meantime we'll have to use library computers.

Even though I don't have a computer in my room, you'll still be able to communicate with the real world with pretty good privacy. I have my own phone! That means you won't need to worry about my parents eavesdropping.

Since you will be here for the whole summer, bring some books along. I have a few books and plenty of magazines that I keep in a magazine stand by my window. There's room enough in it for any books you bring as long as you don't bring too many.

I guess that's all I have to tell except my room only has one bed that we'll have to fight for, unless you bring a sleeping bag. I don't mind taking turns sleeping in it if you want.

That's it. It's a pretty comfortable room. Even though it doesn't have a computer, you can chat with me. Get it? That's a joke. Chat. Chat room. Oh well.

See you soon.

make the connection
to your writing

Before you try a few 1-2-3 maps
and essays of your own, revisit
each sample and look for the writing strategies used by some of the
writers:

- questions that grab audience
  attention
- sentence variety
- effective transitions from one
  paragraph to the next
- effective word choice
- titles reflective of the entire essay

Good writers are always thinking about ways to make their writing interesting. They know that 1-2-3 maps are an organized set of words that
become quality essays because of writing strategies purposefully and effectively selected and executed. In the next chapter you will read about writing
strategies like those mentioned above. For now, it's your turn to try it out.
Write on!

activity 1: cyclical 1-2-3 map

Cereal Essay #4:

Describe a typical day in the life of a teenager. (Description)

directions

1. use the cyclical map you completed in Chapter Three
2. add the box and cylinder to set up your 1-2-3 map; fill the shapes in with words appropriate to your essay topic's objective
3. write your essay following your 1-2-3 map

activity 2: "my room"

Use the word web you prepared in Chapter Two for your room, complete a 1–2–3 map, and use it to write your essay for the prompt:

Your cousin is visiting from out of town and will be staying with you for a week. Write an essay that describes your room so that your cousin will know what to expect.

activities 3, 4, 5, 6: pizza!

Prepare 1-2-3 maps and write essays for each of the prompts in Chapter Three concerning the subject pizza, for which you have already prepared visual maps. Be sure to add the necessary shapes to complete each of your 1-2-3 maps, and conduct mental or written braintalks *before* writing your essays.

- There should be space for you to add a box and cylinder above and below the visual maps you have already completed. If there isn't, attach Post-its™ or paper shapes, which you can tape to your original maps as needed.
- Write words and phrases in the shapes you draw to reflect the essay's main objective, e.g., *describe room for cousin*.
- Examine your visual maps carefully, looking for organizational patterns you might be able to use to identify like subtopics with numbers, check marks, circling, whatever makes sense to you.

alternative assignment lesson

IF YOU FAIL to complete all of the above writing assignments, you will need to write the following statement one hundred times: *The more essays I write, the better at essay writing I become.*

The Good, the Bad, and the Ugly:
Winning and Losing Essays

in Chapter Four, you completed a variety of 1-2-3 Maps and essays for each kind of writing. But the question is: Do the essays demonstrate writing proficiency and to what extent? Another way of putting it is: *Are they good, bad, or ugly?*

You need some constructive feedback that starts with a self-assessment of your own writing skills. Understanding the rubrics introduced in Chapter Two will help you. They are *Idea and Content; Organization; Voice; Word Choice; Sentence Fluency; Conventions/Mechanics.*

In this chapter you will learn about rubrics—the rules and essential principles of good writing. You will learn to work with rubrics, so that they can work *for* you when you write; you will understand each rubric in general and how they relate to your writing in particular. And you will understand how and why *visual writing* helps you with all the aspects of good writing, not just organization.

In other words this chapter makes you ready: *essay test* ready!

organization: the name of the writing game

WHETHER YOU LIVE in Bangor, Maine, or Honolulu, Hawaii, rubrics are the rules that are used to determine or assess your grade in writing. While the terminology of rubrics may vary slightly depending on where you live, *organization*, the first of six rubrics we will explore, is the most important.

Read the following objective for writing assessment from the National Assessment of Educational Progress, NAEP, the people who oversee the most notable writing assessment tests in our country, as well as publish *The Nation's Report Card*:

> Students should display effective choices in the organization of their writing. They should include details to illustrate and elaborate their ideas, and use appropriate conventions of written English.★

With its emphasis on organization, this quote clearly illustrates how your writing success is almost guaranteed when you rely on the principles of visual writing that guide your essay's organization.

organization rules!

YOU WILL LEARN and understand rubrics by using them. Let's examine the two essay samples from the previous chapter whose topic was the nutritional value of a cereal breakfast. Remember: Each student worked from the same hierarchical map.

★Writing Framework and Specifications for the 1998 National Assessment of Educational Progress, National Assessment Governing Board, p. 27.

1-2-3 maps and organization

Here are essential characteristics or traits that define the term *organization* on most rubrics:

- inviting introduction
- thoughtful transitions
- logical, effective sequencing
- controlled pacing
- smooth flow throughout text
- satisfying conclusion

student sample 1

"the breakfast of champions"

How do you choose your breakfast foods? Do you want convenience, and so you choose a Pop-Tart® kind of food? Or do you want nutrition and therefore choose a cereal breakfast? That's what I do, and I do it for three reasons: Carbohydrates, vitamins, minerals, and protein.

Cereal is a major source of carbohydrates. By the time you reach junior high school, you know that carbohydrates provide the body with the energy it needs to function. Our bodies do not do anything without carbohydrates. Thinking, running, writing, and everything else the body does requires energy, and cereal provides it.

If you take a look at the side of any cereal box, you will see a breakdown of its vitamins and minerals. There are a lot of them too, and they are all good for your body. But the best mineral a cereal breakfast contains is calcium. That's because of the milk you add to your cereal. You don't eat it dry, do you? How often have you been reminded by your parents to drink your milk? It's good for your bones. Well they're right. As teenagers, we need to remember our bones; they're still growing. If we don't supply them with foods like milk, then we risk breaking our bones or not developing them properly. Most of us drink Coke or Pepsi during the day, so it just makes sense to add milk to your cereal so you get your calcium.

Besides calcium, the milk you pour on your cereal is also a good protein source. The cereal has a little protein too, but the milk has more. Protein is an essential nutrient that maintains, repairs, and builds our muscles. It's even good for our blood.

By now you know about the nutritional benefits a cereal breakfast supplies. It will start your day off right with a blast of energy. Cereal gives you strong bones. When you eat it with milk you get calcium in addition to all the vitamins and minerals that the cereal and milk have for your body. And finally, a cereal breakfast helps your muscles stay fit because of its protein. There you have it. Cereal really is the "breakfast of champions."

the verdict for sample 1

1. *Inviting Introduction*

The writer invited the reader into her essay with questions before she identified her topic: *"How do you choose your breakfast foods? Do you want convenience and so you choose a Pop-Tart® kind of food? Or do you want nutrition and therefore choose a cereal breakfast?"* The writer skillfully answered her own questions, using the subconcepts laid out in her hierarchical chart: *"Carbohydrates, vitamins and minerals, and protein."* Using topic cues from the box section of her 1-2-3 map as her guide, she introduces her objective, her thesis statement about the nutrition found in cereal, and invites the reader into her essay.

2. *Thoughtful Transition/Logical/Effective Sequencing/Controlled Pacing/Smooth Flow Throughout Text*

You can readily see how this writer used the details from her hierarchical chart, the middle section of her 1-2-3 map. As a result, her essay measures up to the rubric traits that expect *sequenc-*

ing to be *logical* and *effective*. She carries the logic of her chart into her writing and connects the details with style, helping her sentences and paragraphs flow effectively, from one to another.

3. *Satisfying Conclusion*

The ending is satisfying. "There you have it. Cereal really is the breakfast of champions." The writer used the last section of her 1-2-3 map to remind herself that an essay restates the purpose. Rather than a blunt restatement, the writer uses what she knows about good writing, crafting a *satisfying conclusion* by quoting a popular cereal slogan.

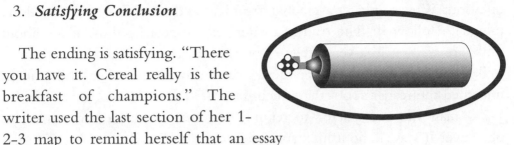

student sample 2:

"cereal"

Cereal is a very nutritious food. When you add milk to it, it's an excellent source of many nutrients. I will discuss the nutrients in a corn flakes and milk breakfast. They are carbohydrates, vitamins, minerals, and protein. Milk provides protein, which builds our muscles. Cereal has some protein but not as much as milk. Crabohydrates are important because they give our bodies energy. Vitamins and minerals are important because they maintain all our bodies' functions. Calcium, which is a mineral found in milk, is very important for strong bones.

1. *Inviting Introduction—NO!*

If this essay were on trial, its defense would not be strong enough to win the case! In a most boring fashion, this writer merely tells the reader that cereal is nutritious. Rather than apply the words in the box of the 1-2-3 map as a guide, he merely recopied them: *"I will discuss the nutrients in a corn flakes and milk breakfast. They are carbohydrates, . . . "*

2. *Thoughtful Transition/Sequencing–Logical/Effective Pacing Controlled/Flows Smoothly*

Not one of these four traits for organization is evident. This essay begs the question: Why construct a graphic organizer and a 1-2-3 map if you don't intend to follow it? The student's statements, especially those made about milk, are written in a very arbitrary way; information about the calcium in milk is in the last sentence when several sentences earlier, the student informed the reader about the protein in milk. Didn't he remember that his 1-2-3 map was constructed to remind him that he needed to restate his objective? It wasn't about milk and calcium.

3. *Satisfying Conclusion*

Satisfying? There isn't even a conclusion to evaluate! The writer did not follow his 1-2-3 map and leaves his readers and his essay hanging.

use it or lose it!

IF YOU PREPARE graphic organizers for the topics laid out by essay prompts, if you construct 1-2-3 maps because you understand how they remind you of essential beginning, middle, and ending statements or paragraphs, please *use* them! Visual maps are not the end; they are the means to the end. Here's how *The Nation's Report Card* experts say it:

> Students may express their ideas and organize their response in an outline, list, word web or other means. With the time constraints in mind, **students should then move to the stage of composition,** during which they draft the material in sentence and paragraph form.★

★Writing Framework and Specifications for the 1998 National Assessment of Educational Progress, National Assessment Governing Board, p. 27.

plan the play and play your plan

YOU HAVE A large reading audience: parents, teachers, state officials, and national organizations like NAEP. With visual writing, you will be ready for them all, no matter what the reason for their interest in your work.

Plan your essay's strategy through visual writing; then, please play your plan. Now that you've familiarized yourself with the rubric for organization, you are ready to continue.

organization: the springboard of effective writing

LET'S TAKE A different, *graphic*, look at the six rubrics as well as NAEP's writing assessment objective, whose hierarchy began with organization: *Students should display effective choices in the organization of their writing. They should include details to illustrate and elaborate their ideas, and use appropriate conventions of written English:*

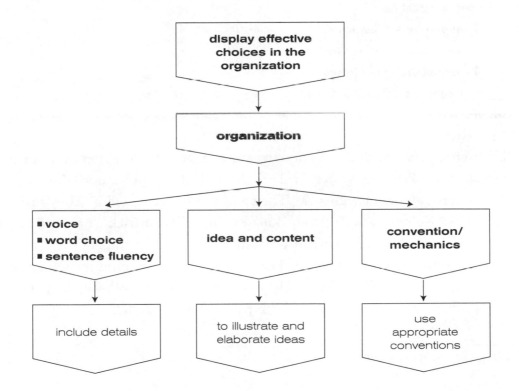

The more you understand the characteristics for each rubric, the more you appreciate the importance of organization!

tools of style:
voice, word choice, sentence fluency

Word Choice

▶ specific and accurate

▶ creates specific pictures

▶ effective verbs, nouns, etc.

▶ precise use of words

Voice

▶ strong, engaging interaction between reader and writer

▶ appropriate for purpose and audience

▶ reflects strong, honest commitment to topic

Sentence Structure

▶ strong, varied, purposeful

▶ well-constructed sentences

▶ natural dialogue (if used)

▶ fragments, *if used,* add style

Word choice, voice, and sentence structure are the tools writers use. Like teenagers on skateboards, some ride them with the hope of not falling off. And others ride them with *style.* They add twists, turns, ollies. They make their tricks seem so easy. And they don't execute all their tricks at once. They add style. They know friends are watching; they have an audience and they want to connect to that audience. They organize in their mind the sequence of the tricks they will perform. They connect them smoothly with transitional moves, all to the delight of both performer and audience.

writing style—the details that score

Like the masters of skateboards, good writers pay attention to their reading audiences. They organize the ideas and details their visual maps present. They refrain from presenting them all at once. Like the skateboard artist, they link their ideas together, connecting them smoothly with purposeful transitional words and sentences, indeed, to the delight of writer and audience.

Looking back to Sample 1, you should be able to recognize how the writer used her natural teenage voice to connect with her peers and how the words and sentences she chose contributed to her overall skillful completion of this essay.

Sample 2 displays little if any sense of voice, word choice or sentence fluency: *"I will discuss the nutrients in a corn flakes and milk breakfast. They are carbohydrates, vitamins, minerals, and protein."*

How might this student have written his thesis statement with attention to these three important rubrics? The writer of Sample 1 did it this way: *"How do you choose your breakfast foods? Do you want convenience and so you choose a Pop-Tart® kind of food? Or do you want nutrition and therefore choose a cereal breakfast? That's what I do and I do it for three reasons: Carbohydrates, vitamins, minerals, and protein."*

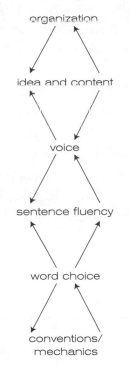

As you can see, working with rubrics isn't that difficult!

idea and content

- ▶ **narrow topic**
- ▶ **fresh, original ideas**
- ▶ **relevant quality details**
- ▶ **accurate, supportive details**

THE CHARACTERISTICS FOR Idea and Content, especially *fresh and original ideas* really do reflect the writer's goal to *illustrate and elaborate ideas.* But how do good writers elaborate their ideas? Here's what *The Nation's Report Card* experts look for:

> One important aspect of the writing process is the student's ability to incorporate effective supportive material into a given piece of writing. The selection of quotations, examples, anecdotes, and other forms of detail show the writer's expertise in choosing material that enriches a given writing task. The choices a writer makes and the explanations attached to those choices, provide insight into the writer's ability to synthesize ideas.★

If you reread Sample 1, you will see that the writer understands the importance of including *effective supportive material.* Besides quoting *"breakfast of champions,"* she uses an anecdote about the importance of drinking milk: *"How often have you been reminded by your parents to drink your milk? It's good for your bones."* She uses several examples that address her defined audience, her peers, for example, *"By the time you reach junior high school, you know that carbohydrates provide the body with the energy . . . "*

★Writing Framework and Specifications for the 1998 National Assessment of Educational Progress, National Assessment Governing Board, p. 27.

conventions/mechanics

- spelling
- grammar
- usage
- paragraphing
- capitalization

THERE IS ONE rubric that is easier to explain than the others: Conventions/Mechanics. Translated, this means spelling, grammar, and correct usage of troublesome words like *too*, *to*, and *two*. These are the things that this rubric pays attention to. The NAEP quote states that writers should "use appropriate conventions of written English." Of course we should. The harder we work on *what* we write, the more we should care about *how* we present it.

If you look back at Samples 1 and 2, you will see a big difference in the quality of the mechanical skills of the two students. While Sample 1 displays few if any errors, Sample 2 has several errors: "carbohydrates" is misspelled in one place while correctly in another; "its" is misused; and there is a fragment in the last statement. Considering the nature of the errors, this writer should have spotted and corrected at least two of them during a careful proofreading. Still, a few errors aren't too bad, which leads us to another aspect of scoring with rubrics. How do rubrics generate scores?

i don't care about rubrics . . . what's my grade?

GOOD TEACHERS TRY to help young writers master the craft of writing by training them to understand and use rubrics. But their young writers are students, after all. And students want to know their grades.

Scoring with rubrics is different from percentages or letter grades. Some schools give numerical grades based on 1 to 4, with 4 the equivalent of *proficiency* or passing. Many schools, however, model their scoring systems after NAEP's suggested six-point scale, with six meaning excellent or advanced, five skilled or strong, and four still signifying proficiency.

writer's checklists

Very often essay test directions include a *Writer's Checklist* made up of guiding questions that are meant to help you evaluate your essays. USE THEM! You will increase your writing skills as well as your insight into what scorers are scoring!

On the next pages you will see examples of what writing levels or grades look like, what rubrics and grades look like together, and then you'll read examples of the kind of questions appearing on Writer's Checklists.

first impressions count!

When climbing the score ladder to success, first impressions very definitely count. School districts often prohibit teachers from scoring their own students' writings. They believe that anonymity helps teachers grade more objectively. Actually, it's true. There's not a teacher out there who hasn't deciphered meaning from confusing text, because they knew the child who wrote it and used that knowledge in a kind of, "This was confusing, but I know what they meant" kind of way. That's another reason to harness organization: Scorers hate being confused by essays they're *forced* to read. So organize! Stay away from your scorer's bad side!

rubric score sheet*

SCORE	Idea and Content	Organization	Voice	Word Choice	Sentence Fluency	Conventions/Mechanics
6-Advanced	Exceptionally clear. Focused. Interesting.	Effective and strong sequencing.	Exceptionally engaging and expressive.	Exceptionally precise and and interesting.	Consistently strong, expressive, and varied.	Very few errors. Barely noticeable.
5-Skilled	Consistently strong. Effective sequencing.	Strong. Effective sequencing.	Expressive and engaging.	Precise and interesting.	Strong and varied.	Few errors.
4-Sufficient	Clear, focused.	Sequencing clear, but may be formulaic.	Occasionally expressive and engaging.	Functional and appropriate to task.	Somewhat varied.	Readable in spite of minor errors.
3-Uneven	Overly general and predictable. Occasionally off-topic.	Inconsistent. Undeveloped. Obvious.	Inappropriately personal or impersona with reading audience.	Ordinary. Lacking precision.	Occasionally awkward.	Limited control. Errors begin to prevent readability.
2-Insufficient	Somewhat unclear. Minimal development.	Lacking consistency and coherence.	Mostly flat, or overly personal or impersonal	Monotonous and/or misused.	Awkward and rambling.	Little control. Frequent and significant errors prevent readability.
1-Unsatisfactory	Lacks central idea. Minimal or no development. Unclear ideas.	Lacking coherence. Disjointed.	Flat. No sense of audience awareness.	Extremely limited. Vague. Imprecise.	Incomplete. Rambling or awkward. Obscured meaning.	Numerous errors seriously prevent readability. Need for extensive editing.

*This chart was developed using *Arizona's Official Scoring Guide for AIMS*, a six-point, six-trait analytic rubric.

rubrics

Definitions of the rubric categories are listed below.

idea and content

Narrow topic/fresh original ideas/relevant quality details/accurate supportive details

organization

Inviting introduction/thoughtful transitions/logical, effective sequencing/pacing controlled/smooth flow/satisfying conclusion

voice

Strong interaction between reader and writer/appropriate for purpose and audience/reflects strong commitment to topic

word choice

Specific and accurate/creates pictures/effective verbs, nouns, etc./precise use of words

sentence fluency

Well-constructed sentences/strong, varied, purposeful structure/natural dialogue if applicable/fragments, if any, add style

conventions/mechanics

Spelling/grammar/usage/paragraphing/capitalization/punctuation/
penmanship

make the connection to your writing

WHAT CAN WRITERS do to improve their writing skills and scores?
Use this 1-2-3 map and descriptions from the rubric score sheet on the
previous page to write an essay that describes a writer's progression from
unsatisfactory to *advanced*.

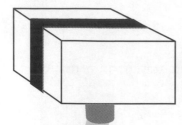

**writer's progression
from 1 to 6**

6-advanced
5-skilled
4-sufficient
3-uneven
2-insufficient
1-unsatisfactory

writer's progression from 1 to 6

make the connection to your writing

USE THE RUBRIC SCORE SHEET TO HELP YOU COMPLETE THE FOLLOWING ACTIVITIES.

- Evaluate the essays you have written so far.
- Evaluate the remaining cereal essays as well as the one entitled "My Room" located in Chapter Three.
- Examine each of the 1-2-3 maps for these essays and assess whether they were used properly.

Tips Before You Start

▶ Reread the essays and analyses of Samples 1 and 2.

▶ Use the following guiding questions to assist you.

Guiding Questions

1. Can you underline examples, anecdotes, and quotations the writer used to support his topic? If not, what might the writer have used?
2. Does the writer have a clear beginning, middle, and end?
3. Does the writer use a variety of sentences or are they all statements? If not, what sentences might be improved upon by revising them to interrogatory, exclamatory, or imperative sentences?
4. Does the writer use exact language or words that seem unclear? Are there any mechanical errors that should be corrected?

writing the good essay

THE MORE YOU experience reading, drafting, and evaluating essays, the better you are at writing them. Also, you can better understand what scorers look for in good writing and, as a result, what good writing is all about. In fact, you will come to appreciate the value of visual writing. Organization, the kind you achieve using graphic organizers and 1-2-3 maps, allows writers the freedom to render visual writing into effectively-written prose: better known as quality essays!

good essays *begin here* . . .

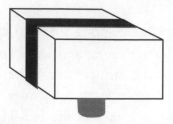

gain momentum in the
middle . . .

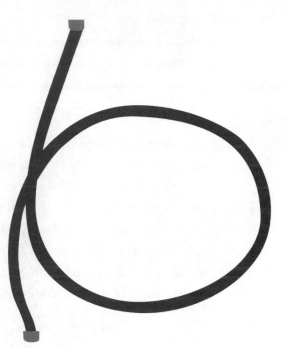

and *end* with ORGANIZATION!

six

Reading and Writing Practice Challenges

there is no better way to finish your journey through *Visual Writing* than by seeing how it works beyond the activities you have created in this book. Chapter Six includes five sections, which invite you to experience authentic essay prompts in a variety of ways.

- Section 1. Prompts and 1-2-3 Maps
- Section 2. Prompts and Essay Responses
- Section 3. Prompts, Essay Responses, plus their 1-2-3 Maps

- Section 4. NAEP 8th grade Prompts, Student Responses from the 1998 Writing Assessment Tests, plus Scorers' Commentaries
- Section 5. Essay Prompts

Are you up for the challenge? If you've gotten this far, it will be as easy as . . . well, you know.

section 1: prompts and 1-2-3 maps

IN THIS SECTION you will read prompts that were presented to students in grades seven through nine. You will also see the 1-2-3 maps that students constructed based on these prompts.

Your challenge: Write essays for each of the prompts using information provided by the 1-2-3 maps shown.

TIME YOURSELF! For each essay, give yourself no more than 25 minutes.

section 2: prompts and essay responses

THIS SECTION PROVIDES you with a different look. You will read authentic essay prompts and a variety of sample essays.

Your challenge: Analyze each prompt and essay sufficiently enough to recreate the 1-2-3 maps from which each essay might have evolved.

By doing so you will have concrete evidence of how well each student accomplished what all good essays must: a satisfying beginning, middle, and end.

TIME YOURSELF! Once again, we will use the time limit that NAEP assessment tests give students to prepare outlines as well as rough drafts: 25 minutes.

section 3: prompts, essay responses,
plus 1-2-3 maps

THIS SECTION PROVIDES you with a complete look at authentic essay prompts, visual maps, and essays they generated. Examine the prompts and evaluate the effectiveness of the maps and their essays. Use the guidelines and rubric chart from Chapter Five to assist you.

Several samples include brief evaluations to help you get started. But the more you use your own analytical style, the more productive this section will be. Preparing multiple copies of the guidelines, rubric chart, and whatever else you find useful, will help you get the most out of this section.

section 4: *the nation's report card* prompts and essays

national assessment of educational progress (NAEP)

IF YOU'VE EVER wondered how your teacher's essay topics and prompts differ from nationally prepared standardized essay tests, this section is for you. You will notice that the official Scorer's Commentary appears after each essay presented in this section. These essays represent work that is completed in 25 minutes, and the scorers are therefore advised to consider the works as drafts rather than final copies.

NAEP scorers use *focused holistic scoring*, which means they rate the overall quality of the writing, focusing their attention on specific characteristics—organization, development, syntax, mechanics★—of student writing that should look very familiar to you by now. Remember that scores range from one (unsatisfactory) to six (advanced). Whether you examine the rubric traits as a whole or individually, good writing begins with a clear game plan—the kind you get from visual writing using 1-2-3 maps with graphic organizers.

★NAEP FACTS, November 2000. U.S. Department of Education, p. 1.

section 5: essay prompts

THIS SECTION PROVIDES what all good writers want and need: practice. There is no better way to improve your writing skills than through practice. The challenge suggested is that you try to complete your visual writing and an essay draft within 25 minutes. Unless you are taking a real NAEP test, you will probably have more time to work on your draft so that it becomes final copy quality. By timing yourself, however, you force your critical thinking skills into high gear. If you are forced to think quickly, you can train yourself to capitalize on the stress your body feels when dealing with time constraints. Your brain's left and right hemispheres function more productively under moderate amounts of stress. And, as you'll remember from Chapter Two, left and right brain cooperation and collaboration is exactly what you need to craft visual maps and quality essays.

> The pace is often frantic for students rushing to organize and write essays. It is no surprise then that their graphic organizers and 1-2-3 maps are often messy, since writing is often a wonderfully messy process.

section 1: prompts and 1-2-3 maps

WRITE ESSAYS FOR each of the prompts using information provided by the 1-2-3 maps completed by each student. If you are familiar with the subject, you may add details to the maps before starting. For each essay, give yourself no more than 25 minutes.

NOTE$_1$—Each prompt and 1-2-3 map came from a unit entitled "Nature's Fury." Besides being an interesting writing subject, these examples were selected because the theme of nature and its impact on man is an objective in most, if not all, state social studies standards.

NOTE$_2$—When a different font appears in a 1-2-3 map, it represents words or phrases, usually insightful, which were added by students after reflecting on their graphic organizers during braintalks or follow-up braintalks.

descriptive

ESSAY PROMPT 1: **Sometimes nature is destructive. But at other times as when leaves, rain, or snow fall, it can be beautiful, and peaceful. Using prose or poetry, describe one of nature's wonders.**

narrative

ESSAY PROMPT 2: **Have you ever experienced nature's fury? People describe their ordeals during earthquakes, hurricanes, and storms with the word "unforgettable." Write a story, real or imagined, in which you or a character you create, experience one form of nature's fury.**

informative

ESSAY PROMPT 3: **Most of the time, man works in harmony with nature. Sometimes that harmony is disturbed by nature's fury, which can result in violent natural disasters. Select at least two natural disasters and explain how nature's fury impacts man's relationship with nature.**

ESSAY PROMPT 4: **Nature's fury comes in many different forms. Choose two natural disasters and describe their differences and similarities.**

ESSAY PROMPT 5: **When man encounters nature without the interference from its destructive side, both nature and man benefit. Choose and explain one of these harmonious cycles.**

persuasive

ESSAY PROMPT 6: **The great French writer and philosopher Voltaire stated: "Men can argue but nature acts." Write a persuasive essay that reflects your agreement or disagreement with this statement.**

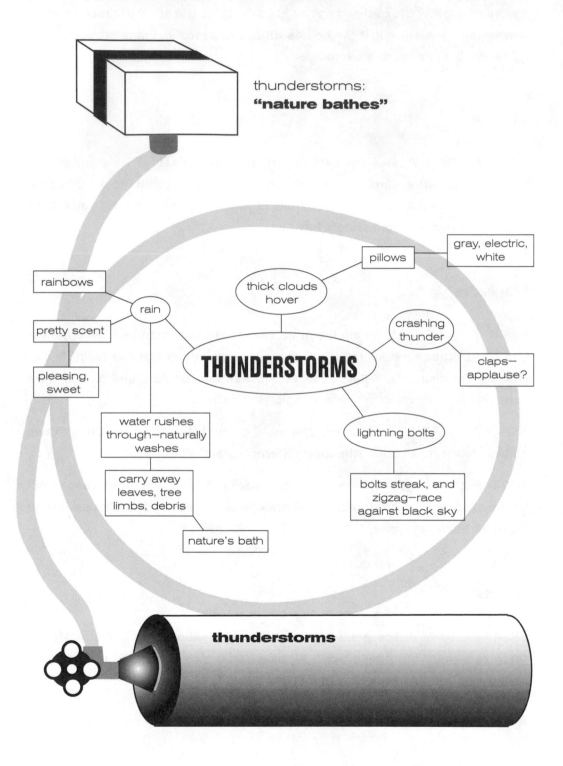

thunderstorms:
"nature bathes"

rainbows

thick clouds hover

pillows — gray, electric, white

rain

pretty scent

pleasing, sweet

THUNDERSTORMS

crashing thunder — claps— applause?

water rushes through—naturally washes

lightning bolts

carry away leaves, tree limbs, debris

bolts streak, and zigzag—race against black sky

nature's bath

thunderstorms

ESSAY PROMPT 2: **Have you ever experienced nature's fury? People describe their ordeals during earthquakes, hurricanes, and storms as unforgettable. Write a story, real or imagined, in which you or a character you create experience one form of nature's fury.**

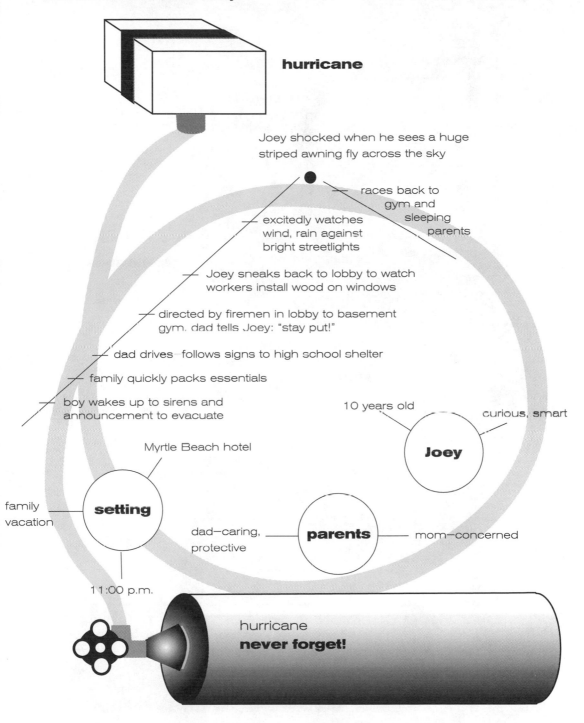

hurricane

Joey shocked when he sees a huge striped awning fly across the sky

races back to gym and sleeping parents

excitedly watches wind, rain against bright streetlights

Joey sneaks back to lobby to watch workers install wood on windows

directed by firemen in lobby to basement gym. dad tells Joey: "stay put!"

dad drives — follows signs to high school shelter

family quickly packs essentials

boy wakes up to sirens and announcement to evacuate

10 years old

curious, smart

Joey

Myrtle Beach hotel

family vacation

setting

dad—caring, protective

parents

mom—concerned

11:00 p.m.

hurricane
never forget!

ESSAY PROMPT 3: **Most of the time, man works in harmony with nature. Sometimes that harmony is disturbed by nature's fury, which can result in sudden and often violent natural disasters. Select at least two natural disasters and explain how nature's fury impacts man's relationship with nature.**

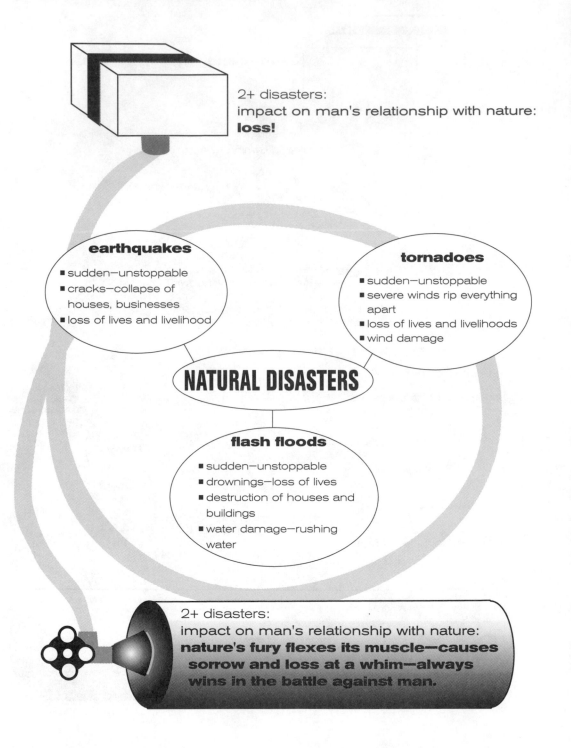

2+ disasters:
impact on man's relationship with nature:
loss!

earthquakes
- sudden—unstoppable
- cracks—collapse of houses, businesses
- loss of lives and livelihood

tornadoes
- sudden—unstoppable
- severe winds rip everything apart
- loss of lives and livelihoods
- wind damage

NATURAL DISASTERS

flash floods
- sudden—unstoppable
- drownings—loss of lives
- destruction of houses and buildings
- water damage—rushing water

2+ disasters:
impact on man's relationship with nature:
nature's fury flexes its muscle—causes sorrow and loss at a whim—always wins in the battle against man.

ESSAY PROMPT 4: **Nature's fury comes in many different forms. Choose two natural disasters and describe their differences and similarities.**

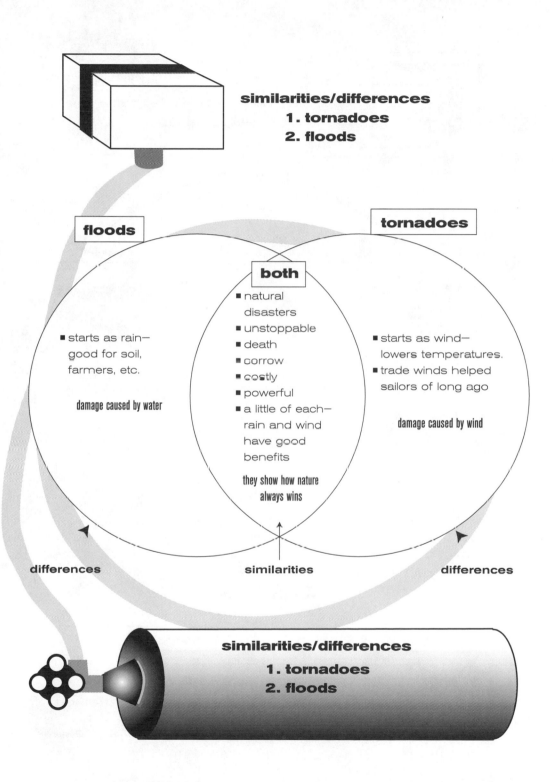

similarities/differences
1. **tornadoes**
2. **floods**

floods

tornadoes

both
- natural disasters
- unstoppable
- death
- corrow
- costly
- powerful
- a little of each—rain and wind have good benefits

they show how nature always wins

- starts as rain—good for soil, farmers, etc.

damage caused by water

- starts as wind—lowers temperatures.
- trade winds helped sailors of long ago

damage caused by wind

differences

similarities

differences

similarities/differences
1. **tornadoes**
2. **floods**

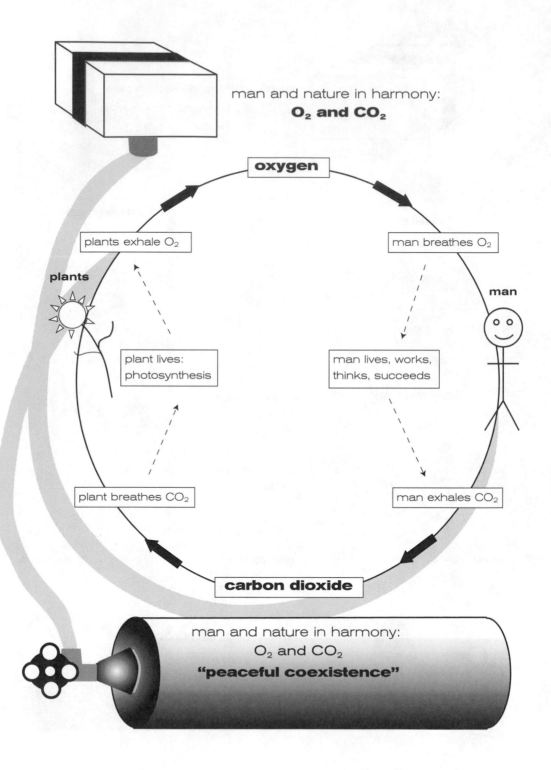

man and nature in harmony:
O₂ and CO₂

oxygen

plants exhale O₂

man breathes O₂

plants

man

plant lives:
photosynthesis

man lives, works,
thinks, succeeds

plant breathes CO₂

man exhales CO₂

carbon dioxide

man and nature in harmony:
O₂ and CO₂
"peaceful coexistence"

ESSAY PROMPT 6: The great French writer and philosopher Voltaire stated: "Men can argue but nature acts." Write a persuasive essay that reflects your <u>agreement</u> or <u>disagreement</u> with this statement.

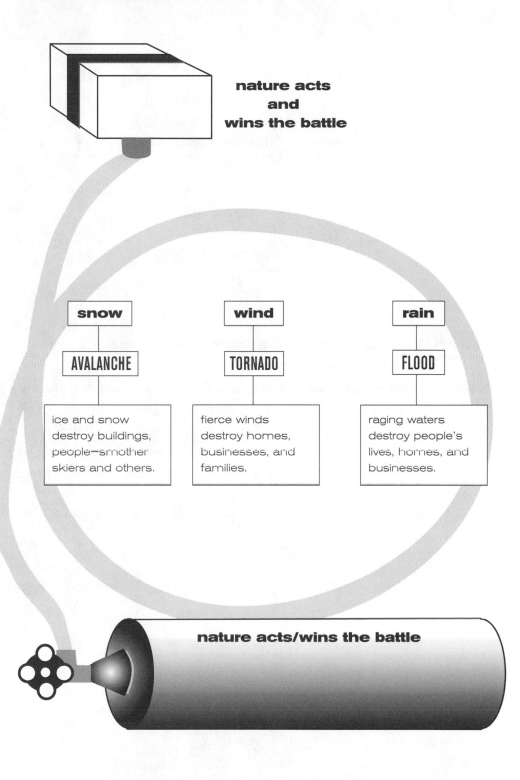

nature acts
and
wins the battle

snow

AVALANCHE

ice and snow destroy buildings, people—smother skiers and others.

wind

TORNADO

fierce winds destroy homes, businesses, and families.

rain

FLOOD

raging waters destroy people's lives, homes, and businesses.

nature acts/wins the battle

Follow-up braintalk: All of nature's fury comes suddenly and without warning. It's costly in so many ways. When nature acts, it's unstoppable, deadly, and victorious. Use in opening and closing.

section 2: prompts and essay responses

SUFFICIENTLY ANALYZE EACH essay prompt and essay enough to recreate the 1-2-3 maps from which each essay evolved.

NOTE: Your 1-2-3 maps will match each essay's content, so for each essay you must ask yourself: *Does this essay have a satisfying beginning, middle, and end?* If not, add sections to the map that would have completed it, thereby improving the map and, more importantly, the essay.

TIME YOURSELF! For each essay, spend no more than 25 minutes.

soccer

Listen to what happens! The ball glides swiftly through the air. A player slides across the ground to steal the speeding ball. Players run quickly and quietly toward the goal while hearing screams of, "Go! Go! Go!" The ball hits the tightly woven blanket of string. A player dives feet first along the wet ground and trips another player. The referee blows his loud, ear-piercing whistle. A free kick is announced; the player takes three giant steps back and smashes the ball past the goalie into the bright orange net. The muddy shoe slaps the multicolored ball, sending it into the air. The ball hits the goal post and bounces off of it like a spring. The player throws the ball in, and it bounces along the ground. The ball skids into the chalky white lines and is devoured in the powdery white sediment. The goalie's gentle hands catch the fast moving ball. The referee blows his whistle three times, which signals the end of the game.

horses

Watch as they glide across the high green grass. Runner's blood flows through their swaying manes, like wolves running to capture their prey. Mares, stallions, and even colts all run to the same destination as one big cloud scuttles across the sky on a steamy, summery day. Once they reach their destination, it is as if there is a sudden jerk as they all surround the fresh, blue watering hole and start drinking. There isn't an ounce of weariness within them.

operation sleep sac

Look around on the streets and what do you see? Lights? Backed up traffic? Pollution? Besides all of these terrible things you'll see homeless children—children who have to beg for money just so they can live. These children are very unhappy, and need help. And the organization called Operation Sleep Sac is just the way to help these unhappy children.

Operation Sleep Sac is an association designed to accept donations for special people. Operation Sleep Sac gives these wonderful donations to children in need. These donations not only make these children very happy, but they also help the children live.

Without this remarkable organization, some children's lives would turn from bad to absolutely terrible. That's what makes this organization essential—it provides essential materials for poor and poverty-stricken children. If not for Operation Sleep Sac, more children would be begging, and world hunger would be increased instead of decreased. More children would suffer and possibly even die. That's why we need and should support this organization—it does so many good things for so many underprivileged children.

Have you been thinking about the kind of writing exemplified by each of these essays?

▶ Descriptive

▶ Informative

▶ Narrative

▶ Persuasive

---

section 3: prompts, essay responses, plus their 1-2-3 maps

EXAMINE THE PROMPTS and evaluate the effectiveness of the visual maps and essays. Use the guiding questions and rubric chart (Chapter Five) to assist you.

BE CAREFUL! NOT ALL THE STUDENTS IN THIS SECTION USED VISUAL WRITING EFFECTIVELY.

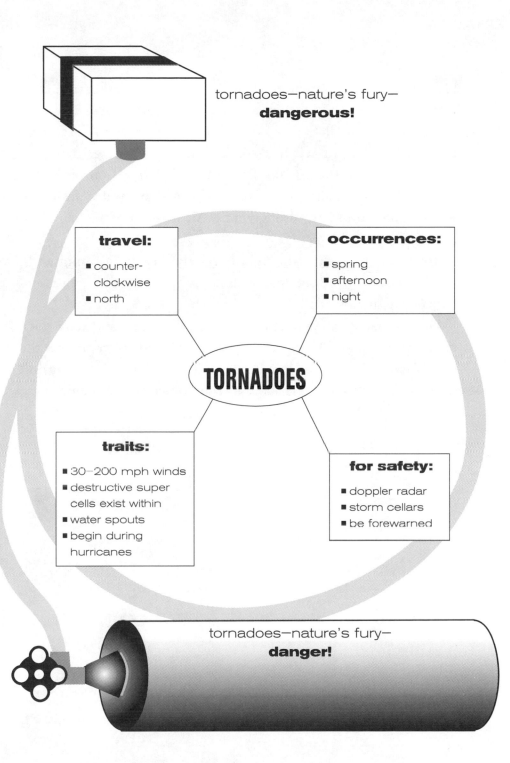

tornadoes—nature's fury—
dangerous!

travel:
- counter-clockwise
- north

occurrences:
- spring
- afternoon
- night

TORNADOES

traits:
- 30–200 mph winds
- destructive super cells exist within
- water spouts
- begin during hurricanes

for safety:
- doppler radar
- storm cellars
- be forewarned

tornadoes—nature's fury—
danger!

ESSAY 1A

tornadoes

Have you ever experienced danger? Like a dangerous thunderstorm? Well, multiply that by ten and you have a tornado.

No one can predict or stop tornadoes. They come in the springtime, afternoons, or when it's dark. They usually travel counterclockwise and to the North. They can either travel on or off the ground, and sometimes on water. Tornadoes on water are called waterspouts. Both have strong winds. A tornado's winds can reach from 30–200 mph!

Tornadoes can begin during a hurricane because of miniswirls, small tornado winds. Super cells are the most dangerous and destructive storms of all.

Doppler radar can predict the speed of the winds and warn people to find shelter. During a dangerous storm, a storm cellar is the best place to be. Being forewarned is the best protection against dangerous storms and tornadoes . . . the outcome can be deadly.

ESSAY PROMPT 1: **Nature's fury comes in many shapes and sizes, often leaving a path of destruction. How do tornadoes exemplify nature's fury?**

ESSAY 1B

nature's fury

Tornadoes, or in other words, death and destruction, are the fastest winds on earth. Tornadoes are the rotating funnel clouds that extend high above clouds. Once these violent winds touch down almost nothing can stop them. They uproot trees, overturn railroad cars, and send automobiles flying like matchbox cars. Side effects from tornadoes are heavy rain, hail, lightning storms, and power outages. There have been hundreds of tornadoes reported annually since 1950, and they have killed over 10,000 people in the United States alone since 1900. Tornadoes, cyclones, and twisters are the most violent and unpredictable natural phenomenon the world has ever seen.

HAVE A LOOK AT THE FOLLOWING 1-2-3 MAP FOR ESSAY 1B

- The 1-2-3 map and outline is created using a word web.
- The map was examined carefully.
- Now use the rubric chart to help you score the essay.

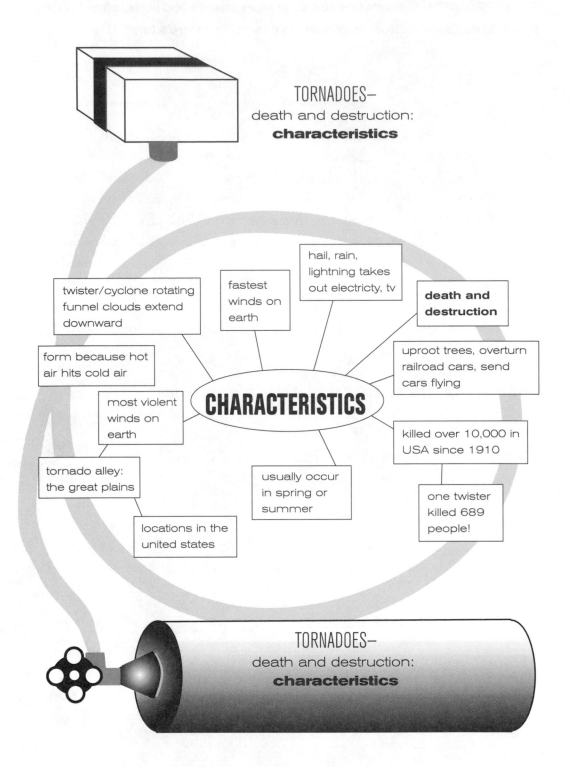

TORNADOES—
death and destruction:
characteristics

twister/cyclone rotating funnel clouds extend downward

fastest winds on earth

hail, rain, lightning takes out electricty, tv

death and destruction

form because hot air hits cold air

CHARACTERISTICS

uproot trees, overturn railroad cars, send cars flying

most violent winds on earth

killed over 10,000 in USA since 1910

tornado alley: the great plains

usually occur in spring or summer

one twister killed 689 people!

locations in the united states

TORNADOES—
death and destruction:
characteristics

ESSAY PROMPT 1: **Nature's fury comes in many shapes and sizes, often leaving a path of destruction. How do tornadoes exemplify nature's fury?**

ESSAY 2: 1-2-3 Map

Look closely at this 1-2-3 Map for Essay 2 because you'll want to avoid problems like these.

No braintalk. No 1-2-3 Map. No follow-up braintalk. Pretty dangerous. There's one more problem. You will notice that the outline sometimes uses sentences. Avoid this practice! The tendency, especially when nervous, is to transfer sentences from outline to essay, producing essays devoid of adequate voice, word choice, spelling errors, and sentence fluency.

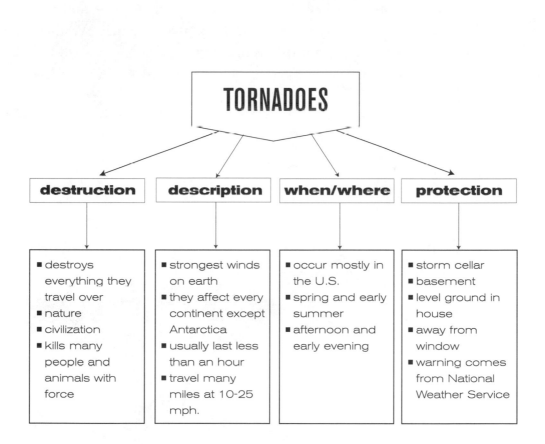

TORNADOES

destruction	**description**	**when/where**	**protection**
■ destroys everything they travel over ■ nature ■ civilization ■ kills many people and animals with force	■ strongest winds on earth ■ they affect every continent except Antarctica ■ usually last less than an hour ■ travel many miles at 10-25 mph.	■ occur mostly in the U.S. ■ spring and early summer ■ afternoon and early evening	■ storm cellar ■ basement ■ level ground in house ■ away from window ■ warning comes from National Weather Service

ESSAY 2

The strongest winds on earth come from tornadoes at speeds of more then 200 miles per hour. Tornadoes affect every continent except Antarctica. They usually last less then an hour traveling around twenty miles at ten to twenty miles per hour. Tornadoes destroy everything they travel over including civilization and nature. They kill many people and animals with their powerful force. Tornadoes are formed by warm, twisting masses, which form a funnel that reaches downward and usually touches the ground. Tornadoes occur mostly in the Untied States in spring and early summer. They usually strike in the afternoon and early evening. Protection for tornadoes is usually provided by storm cellar, basement, or if you don't have this, a level ground in a home under a bed. Warnings for tornadoes come from the National Weather Service. The force of a tornado is unmatched.

ESSAY PROMPT 1: **Nature's fury comes in many shapes and sizes, often leaving a path of destruction. How do tornadoes exemplify nature's fury?**

Okay, you're on your own! Analyze this 1-2-3 map and the essay. Hint: Be careful!

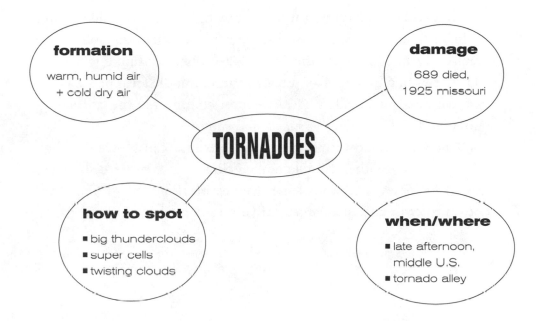

formation

warm, humid air + cold dry air

damage

689 died, 1925 missouri

TORNADOES

how to spot

- big thunderclouds
- super cells
- twisting clouds

when/where

- late afternoon, middle U.S.
- tornado alley

twisters: nature's fury

Tornadoes are massive, twisting, destructive beasts of nature, causing great destruction. Tornadoes can toss anything as if it were a small child's toy. They can flatten objects in their path. With hard rains, they can flood a whole town. And like the deadly tornado of 1925 that ran through Missouri, Illinois, and Indiana with winds up to 280 mph, they can kill hundreds of people. 689 people died in the tornado of 1925.

These beasts of nature form when warm, humid air collides with cold, dry air. The warm air rises and more warm air comes to replace it. In some cases the air starts to rotate causing a tornado. These twisting masses of air usually form in middle areas of the U.S. known as Tornado Alley. They are most common in the late afternoon and early evening of spring and summer.

When a tornado forms, large thunderclouds can be seen in the sky. They are either cumulonimbus clouds or a super cell. The cloud becomes hard and dense. Masses of clouds at the bottom begin to twist and turn, and a tornado is formed.

ESSAY PROMPT 2: **Think about the rules you must follow to succeed at your school. Explain to a new student what those rules are and why they are important to a student's success.**

NOTE: In addition to the above prompt, you can look at the already prepared 1-2-3 map seen below. Use it as the organizational tool. Remember: The 1-2-3 map guides your essay's organization, but you must attend to the five remaining categories in the rubric.

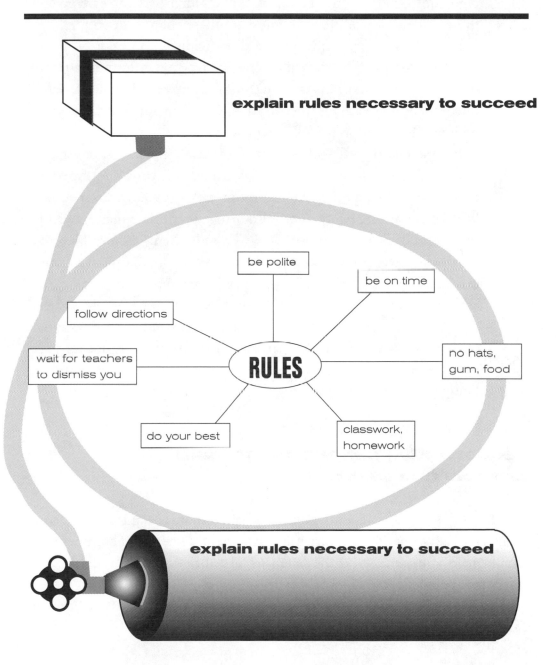

explain rules necessary to succeed

be polite

be on time

follow directions

wait for teachers to dismiss you

RULES

no hats, gum, food

do your best

classwork, homework

explain rules necessary to succeed

rules, rules, rules

Why does the average middle school classroom need rules? The answer is simple. To keep order of course! Because without rules or regulations, there would be chaos, and children wouldn't be given the chance to learn. Now let me share these rules with you.

First of all, respect and care for all individuals and their property. That way, you'll be treated the same way. Next, you must attend school on time and remain seated until dismissed. If you are late once, there is a warning for you. If you are late another time, you will get an afternoon school detention.

Before entering the classroom, discard all food and beverage items unless you feel like spilling grape juice on your new sweater or shorts. Upon entering the classroom, take off your hat, especially all of you young gentlemen. Also bring appropriate materials and supplies. The school cannot always provide them, so it is nice to have your own. Then listen to and follow all directions that your teacher or peers give you, so you won't mess up on a homework assignment or group project. You must use class time wisely. Learn speaking and writing to bring you success. If you have a question, raise your hand and wait for permission to speak, so as not to disturb the learning environment. Last but not least, and most importantly, do your very best.

section 4: *the nation's report card*
prompts and essays

READ THE PROMPTS, eighth grade student responses, and scorers' commentaries, all from NAEP's writing assessment tests. The commentaries should help you understand the language of rubrics as interpreted by very important people: national scorekeepers!

EXTRA CHALLENGE: Review NAEP essays identified as *Excellent* and *Skillful* and produce 1-2-3 maps for each of them.

DESIGNING A TV SHOW

A public television network is seeking ideas for a new series of shows that would be educational for teenagers. The series will include ten one-hour episodes and will be shown once a week. Some of the titles under consideration are:

- "Great Cities of the World"
- "Women in History"
- "Nature Walks"
- "American Legends"

Choose one of these titles. Write a letter to the network president describing your ideas for a new educational series. In your letter, describe what one episode might be like. Use specific examples of what information you would include in the episode so the network president will be able to imagine what the series would be like.

1. Sample "Unsatisfactory" Response

```
Dear President,
   I would like to do a brochure, on "Great Cities of
the World" I need your opinion should I do it on New
York, Tokyo, Tiawan, Los Angelos, or should I do all
of them?
Always
Student
```

SCORER'S COMMENTARY

The "Unsatisfactory" rating was given to 3% of the responses to this topic. As the scoring guide indicates, such responses were undeveloped or very poorly written. In the "Unsatisfactory" response shown above, the student chooses one of the series titles provided in the topic and asks what to include, without presenting his or her ideas about what to show on the television series.

---

*Eighth graders were given a number of topics in 1998. The informative scoring guide was used for all of the topics.

2. Sample "Insufficient" Response

```
Dear President
  I think you should do the series on "Great City's
of the World." If you did the series off of that
title it would be best. You would get to learn about
all the cities instead of just one city. Because
teenagers could learn about other cities in other
countries. That's why I think you should do the
series on "Great City's of the World."
```

SCORER'S COMMENTARY

The "Insufficient" rating was given to 13% of the responses to this topic. Such responses supplied only minimal information about the student's choice of an educational television series. In the example shown above, the student provides a justification for the series: "You would get to learn about all the cities instead of just one city." However, the student does not develop that justification by describing the substance of the show.

3. Sample "Uneven" Response

```
Dear Network President,
  I think you should do a show on American legends.
You can tell about real people like George Washington
or Abraham Lincoln. You might want to consider using
fictional characters such as Paul Bunyan or Johnny
Appleseed. You might want to do shorter section on
all of the less popular Presidents like Teddy
Roosevelt or Woodrow Wilson. I would put in how
George Washington helped win the Revolutionary War
or how he made a good President You could also tell
how John F. Kennedy was assasianated or how Abraham
Lincon helped in the Cival War.
```

SCORER'S COMMENTARY

The "Uneven" rating was given to 40% of the responses to this topic. In many of these responses, students mentioned a few specific elements to be presented on the television series, but listed rather than developed them. In the "Uneven" paper shown above, the student enumerates various

"American Legends" to be presented, along with an identifying detail or two about George Washington, John F. Kennedy, and Abraham Lincoln, for example: "You could also tell how John F. Kennedy was assasianated or how Abraham Lincon helped in the Cival War." The student, however, does not develop points, and his or her command of the mechanics of writing is uneven.

4. Sample "Sufficient" Response

```
Dear Mr. President, I think you should have a show
about "Women in history." A lot of people want to
know about women and what they've done to help our
country. There have been many women heroes, and they
should be recognized. You could do the show like
Wishbone, except all the shows be about women in his-
tory instead of characters from a book. An idea for
a show is Anne Frank. You could go to the place where
they hid for so long and do the show right there.
Everyone will get the chance to see how Anne lived.
A lot of people haven't heard or seen her story.
Well, it's time they do! So, please take into con-
sideration my ideas and respond when you make your
decision.
```

SCORER'S COMMENTARY

Students at the upper score levels ("Sufficient" or better) provided organized responses with illustrative details. Some students provided descriptions of an entire episode, down to the dialogue and camera angles. The "Sufficient" rating was given to 34% of the responses to this topic. Such responses were organized and provided some details. In the response shown above, the student's writing is clear, accurate, and organized.

5. Sample "Skillful" Response

```
Dear Network President,
   I think that I have a new show for your network.
It's called Great Cities of the World. The show is
about four teenagers, around the ages of fourteen to
seventeen who travel around the world. In each show
```

they travel to two cities. When they arrive in the city they will first talk about the city's history and what it is like now in the present. They talk about some of the tradions of the city. For example if the students went to Paris, France, they would talk about France's past and some of the things they do in there daily lives. They could talk about the people, what they look like and their styles. To keep the show interesting you can show things such as we learn how to say a word from their language or meet many different people from their city. Also to keep the show interesting they can have problems.

SCORER'S COMMENTARY

The "Skillful" rating was given to 8% of the responses to this topic. In such responses, students used detail and elaboration in parts of the response, with transitions to connect ideas. In the response shown above, the student specifies who will be the narrators of the show and the order in which information will be presented: "The show is about four teenagers, around the ages of fourteen to seventeen who travel around the world. In each show they travel to two cities. When they arrive in the city they will first talk about the city's history and what it is like now in the present." The student also uses the example of Paris as the subject for one show. The student uses complex sentences and transitions (such as "When they arrive in the city . . . ", "For example . . . .") to tie points together and lead the reader through the essay.

6. Sample "Excellent" Response

Dear Network president,

   Hello! I am a young teenager and I think that teenagers these days would like to see something educational. I think a good idea for a TV show would be "Great Cities of the World." ¶For example, one episode could be about Chicago and tell famous places you could visit. One place could be the Sears Tower in which a camera could show people going up in an elevator and then seeing the view of downtown Chicago. ¶Another place the TV show could go to is the Shed Aquarium. In it are many types of ocean life that interesting to see up close. They could also go to the art museum and look at famous paintings. ¶Just for fun, the show could go to F.A.O. Schwartz, a large toy store with many toys you can play with. As a matter of fact, you could just go shopping period. Chicago is known for its many stores. ¶Then you could take a trip to a restaurant such as Ed Debivic's or Planet Hollywood, just to spice up the show a bit. ¶Now that I've explained where to go in Chicago, I'll tell you a little more about the setup of the show. I think that you should have a host who is young, around fiftheen, energetic, and a spunky personality. He or she could act as the tour guide and show the viewers around each city. She could also explain the city's trademark's, such as the Sears Tower. I think that if you use a young person, it would attract young viewers.

¶ And last of all, I think the camera should look at the city as if it was viewer's eyes. For example, when you look around, you see things as you would see them, as if you were really there in Chicago, sight-seeing.

¶ Well, I hope you enjoy my input and put it into consideration. I'll be looking forward to seeing a new TV show about "Great Cities of the World."

SCORER'S COMMENTARY

The "Excellent" rating was given to 2% of the responses to this topic, in which students used detail and development across the response. The "Excellent" response shown above describes an entire episode of a television series in detail. The student includes such details as how the camera would move: "One place could be the Sears Tower in which a camera could show people going up in an elevator and then seeing the view of downtown Chicago." He or she describes a wide variety of sights in Chicago with suggestions for how to present them. Points such as "I think the camera should look at the city as if it was the viewer's eyes" enable the reader to visualize the show. This student shows good control of language; occasional minor errors do not interfere with meaning. (Note: The "¶" symbols in the sample are paragraph signs and reflect symbols placed in the text by the student.)

NAEP 1998 eighth grade narrative writing assessment

PROMPT

Imagine this situation!

A noise outside awakens you one night. You look out the window and see a spaceship. The door of the spaceship opens, and out walks a space creature. What does the creature look like? What do you do?

Write a story about what happens next.

2. Sample "Insufficient" Response

```
Well the the creature is big and grean with a big
head and big huge eyes in the front and back of this
heard he/she has short arms And has big long legs
with no toes then he shot laser beams into my eyes
I guess so he could read my mind and that is why he
did that Then I invited him into my house so we could
play games.
```

SCORER'S COMMENTARY

This "Insufficient" response has some vivid description of the creature, with "big huge eyes in the front and back of his head." It also includes some dramatic action: "he shot laser beams into my eyes I guess so he could read my mind." The entire lack of punctuation makes it hard to know where sentences begin and end, and so make the story somewhat hard to read throughout. The vocabulary is also rather simple.

3. Sample "Uneven" Response

```
I was ounce awakened by a loud noise outside I got
out of the bed grabbed a flashlight went to the win-
dow lifted the blindes There was a spaceship in my
front yard! I didn't know what to do! Then all of
sudden the door of the spaceship's opened up and out
```

walked a little space creature. He had big eyes, an oval head, and two holes for nostrils. He had a small which was used for eating. He look kind of freindly. He go of the spaceship walked my window, Then he held up two fingers and I knew he was peaceful. Then he took a picture of me. I went to get my camera, but by the time I got back he was gone, So I just went back to sleep.

SCORER'S COMMENTARY

This "Uneven" response combines some characterization of the space visitor ("He had big eyes, an oval head, and two holes for nostrils") with some very general, imprecise development. The reader is introduced to the "little space creature," but this creature leaves before the tale unfolds much further. Statements such as "He looked kind of friendly" are not followed up in a way that would add to the story's development. Sentence boundaries are unevenly observed; correct sentences such as "I didn't know what to do!" are interspersed with sentences such as "I got out of the bed grabbed a flashlight went to the window lifted the blinds" that have errors in both punctuation and syntax. Overall, the level of sentence control and development make this an "uneven" response to the topic.

4. Sample "Sufficient" Response

The space ship it was about as big as a school. When the door opened an alien stepped out. He had on egg shaped head with black misty eyes, white short body with long arms and three long fingers. He took his helmet off and started talking in some different language. Then he pressed a button and started speaking in english. He said, Greetings earthling, my name is Recabae what is Your Name? My name is Frank, nice to meet you. He asked me if I wanted to go on a journey with him. I said sure. We got in his space craft and shot up through the clouds at 2,000 knots pluse. He asked what I would like to do. I said lets go exploring other Galaxies. We went where no man has gon before. We went to the Condego galaxie. It ha seven suns 12 moons and 54 planets in it's system. We started decending and that's when he said it's time to go home. He dropped me off and then all of a sudden I awoke from my great dream.

SCORER'S COMMENTARY

This "Sufficient" response has a clear beginning, middle, and end, and does apply the general conventions of storytelling. Though the conventions of dialogue are not followed precisely, this writer attempts to add speaking parts to the story to heighten interest. Some nice detail ("We went to the Condegua galaxie. It ha seven suns 12 moons and 54 planets in its system.") is hampered by subtle yet pervasive errors in punctuation and rather thin development of plot. The sentences, for the most part, are simple and unvaried. This response is a good example of a "Sufficient" paper that, though hampered by lack of development and some writing flaws, still tells a story that is clear and relatively detailed.

5. Sample "Skillful" Response

It is 3:30 in the morning and I am sudden awoke by a spaceship that just landed in my backyard. I am very scared, nervous, and excited. The door on the spaceship opens and a dark cloud of smoke pours out of the ship along with a little green space creature. I am not sure what to do, I don't want to screem and wake up everyone in the house and scare off the creature that just landed in my backyard. I sit down on my bed for a minute and think what to do and then I look out my window again. The creature is now going through the garbage cans; I wonder maybe he is hungry:

I run down stairs and make a peanut-butter and jelly sandwhich and go outside. At first the creature is startled by my sudden presence, but then he sees what I have in my hand. He comes running towards my hand, but then I realize he wants the sandwhich. I give it to him and he throws it about twenty feet in the air, and catches it in his mouth and swallows.

The little creature looks at me and smiles, he then says something in some type of foreign language, gets in his ship circles the house and disappears. I never saw the creature again, but some times, really late at night, I could swear I hear someone making a sandwhich in the kitchen!

SCORER'S COMMENTARY

In this "Skillful" response, the writer wittily portrays the space creature, whose primary interest seems to be in a peanut butter and jelly sandwich. There are some errors such as comma splices, and the response does not provide details about the space creature or about the writer's own reactions as consistently or fully as the "Excellent" responses.

6. Sample "Excellent" Response

Crash! A noise awakened my midnight slumber. I looked about frantically, wondering where the noise had come from. Another sound like gas escaping from a soda can. I leap out of the bed and dash to the window. Slowly I part the curtains to what I see almost makes me scream.

Standing about 20 ft. from my window is an alien bathed in purple-blue light. It reminded me of an X-Files alien. At first glance I noticed its prominent black eyes, large, flat nose, well-proportioned lips, high cheekbones, and small, slightly protuding ears. It was also bald. When I looked at it more thoroughly other details come to mind. It looked to be about 5'7" with greenish-white skin, and a strong and limber body. I can only guess as to what its real body was like under it's peach colored space suit.

Slowly it raised its hand and waved to me. I wondered if I should wave back or not and decided to, even though I was scared enough to turn and run screaming down the hallway, but I waved instead.

As I stood there, waving like a fool I began to think really weird things. Things like "Help me save

your planet" and "You must help me." On some sub-
conscious level I realized it was communicating
telepathically. I tried as hard as I could to reply
to but found I could.

Through our telepathic communication I found out I
was supposed to help him save Earth. I noticed he
was now suited in full Armani attire.

I deliberated with myself & decided to help it.
Now as I look back it seems so weird to me. But then
I remember all the fun we had and I reflect upon how
we saved Earth. It was one of the best times of my
life.

SCORER'S COMMENTARY

This "Excellent" response has a dramatic opening: "Crash! A noise awakened my midnight slumber." The student sustains dramatic action throughout the story, and provides precise detail that makes it easy to visualize the space crea-ture: "Standing about 20 ft. from my window is an alien bathed in purple-blue light." The student describes his or her own reaction to heighten sus-pense: " . . . I was scared enough to turn and run screaming down the hall-way, but I waved instead." Although the action in the second part of the story is somewhat telescoped, the response is complete and well developed overall.

NAEP 1998 eighth grade persuasive writing assessment

PROMPT

Many people think that students are not learning enough in school. They want to shorten most school vacations and make students spend more of the year in school. Other people think that lengthening the school year and shortening vacations is a bad idea because students use their vacations to learn important things outside of school.

What is your opinion?

Write a letter to your school board either in favor of or against lengthen-ing the school year. Give specific reasons to support your opinion that will convince the school board to agree with you.

3. Sample "Uneven" Response

Dear School board,

My name is "John Doe" and I think that you should let us keep our vacation as they are. We are doing fine as we are. If you think we're not doing as we are supposed to do then that's your opinion. Besides even if not if you don't do good your vacation is shortened any way because you will have to go to summer school and make your grades up. Even if you don't have to go you can go any way.and you say not all people go to summer school well that's true but mostly who ever doesn't already has good grades or they don't care about it so lengthing it will still be even worse because that gives them more time to make mistakes and lower their grade. In my opinion I would like to have school every other day so that when you go to school one day you might do your homework that night but don't finish it the next day if you don't have school you can finish it and then go play even longer so you will get your A and your play. Also if you want to get us smarter you could just teach us all this stuff at an early age and as we begin to grow we will know high school stuff in the 4th or 5th grade

SCORER'S COMMENTARY

This "Uneven" response presents many reasons for preserving vacations "as they are." The student makes some good points, although he or she does not always express them clearly. He or she notes that, for unmotivated students, "lengthing it will still be even worse because that gives them more time to make mistakes . . . " and points out that it might be more effective to introduce high-school level material in earlier grades. However, the essay is rather rambling, as the student has not structured his or her ideas into a clear or ordered format.

I am a student at [school name]. I belive that the idea for a longer school year and a shorter summer vacation is a wonderful suggestion.

Why you may ask? I feel this way because I personally want to learn more. Like for instance China has a program that their students go to school for six-weeks. Then they are out for two weeks. They do this all through out the year. So it's like they never get a three month break.

Most students, when they get out of school for the summer they forget what they learned the following year. So then their teachers have to go over what they learned.

If we had a shorter summer then we probably would not forget what we learned. And I also feel that when students get out for summer vacation, they do not use their time for thinking about school. All that their interested in is having fun.

SCORER'S COMMENTARY

In this "Sufficient" response, the student provides a clear position in favor of a longer school year. The student cites several examples to support that position, such as the lack of long vacation breaks in China, but the examples are not linked to each other. The control of language is not as strong as in the "Skillful" and "Excellent" responses: "Most students, when they get out of school for the summer they forget what they learned the following year." The student's control of sentence boundaries and paragraph structure, as well as the generally appropriate use of language, make the paper clear overall.

5. Sample "Skillful" Response

Dear School Board,

I think that we should stay in ~~she~~ school for a longer part of the year. I believe this would help us to remember more of what we learned the year before and we would have more time to have classes that begin to teach a trade (for example) in younger years.

Even though I treasure having time off during the summer I don't think that I accomplish anything or need that time. It puts me out of the habit of studying and I lose a lot of knowledge.

If we did stay in school year round we would have some of that extra time to spend on learning a trade as an exploratory. This would give us experience and an idea of some things we might enjoy doing as a proffession later on in life.

These are my thoughts on the year round schooling and many of my peers would argue with it and complain if the year round school idea was used but I feel it would be best.

SCORER'S COMMENTARY

This "Skillful" response develops a clear position for lengthening the school year. This response shows sound development and (with minor exceptions) control over grammar and syntax. The logic and syntactic variety of this response, however, are not as good as in the "Excellent" responses. The writer explains what he or she might accomplish in an extended school year, such as learning a trade. The writer's arguments, however, are slightly less developed and slightly less eloquent than those of the "Excellent" responses.

6. Sample "Excellent" Response

To Whom it May Concern,

I've heard about the debate of whether or not to lengthen the school year. I decided to voice my opinion. I believe that the school year should *not* be lengthened. Kids are stressed out enough with homework and school without adding more. Some might say that kids aren't learning enough, and since the future of the nation rests on their shoulders they need to go to school longer and learn more. I say those who are adults now went to school the same amount, if not shorter, of time that we do and they haven't completely ruined the country.

To make the country better you don't just need to know math, English, and history; you need to know social skills like getting along with others. You learn social skills like getting along with others. You learn social skills at school but you can learn them just as easily while on vacation. If you go to another country for vacation you learn to accept and respect other cultures. This can help extinguish prejudices.

If you add more schoolwork and homework kids will get more stressed out. When you're stressed out you aren't as agreeable and sometimes just give up trying and don't care a difference in the world.

I once heard someone say that you are only a kid for a short time. When you're an adult you have enough stress ~~agre lotof~~ and hardly any time. for fun, so why put stress on kids and make them lose their time for fun. Why turn them into adults before their time?

I completely agree with the person who said this. Let kids have fun and not be stuck in a hot school listening to a lecture, or at home doing homework when they used to be swimming or hanging out with their friends.

Thank you for considering my letter.

SCORER'S COMMENTARY

This student sustains an argument around the idea that lengthening the school year will subject students to additional stress and will result in their losing some opportunities: "You learn social skills at school but you can learn them just as easily while on vacation. If you go to another country for vacation you learn to accept and respect other cultures." The student provides a clear, connected series of reasons to argue persuasively against lengthening the school year. While there are occasional spelling errors, overall the student is adept in varying sentence length and structure, providing evidence to back up his or her point of view. This response was rated "Excellent."

section 5: essay prompts

READ THROUGH THE variety of prompts that follow. Write at least one essay for each kind of writing, *or* write essays for the prompts you find particularly challenging.

Practice writing, especially visual writing. *Remember:* **Writing great essays is as easy as 1-2-3!**

---

descriptive essay prompts

- Just as artists use brushes to paint pictures, writers use words. Choose something you value—a pet, a vacation spot, an object, etc. Using vivid sensory details, describe it for a friend who has never seen it.
- Describe a place where people go to have a good time. Using prose or poetry, describe the place so clearly that someone who has never been there understands what it is like.
- Think of a teacher who you will remember for a long, long time. Using prose or poetry, describe that teacher so clearly that your reader will know just what makes him or her so hard to forget.
- It is often said that beauty is in the eye of the beholder. Think of a scene from nature that fits the quote perfectly, and describe that scene for someone who might never have seen it.

narrative essay prompts

- Young children spend a lot of time waiting for special events. Write a story to your parents describing an event you could hardly wait to begin or end.
- Suppose you woke up one morning to find that there was no electricity. Write a story for future generations of what life is like with this sudden change.

- It is thirty years from now. Your name has just been called, and you are about to receive an award. Write a story to your future children describing your accomplishment.

- "Failure is often a better teacher than success." As someone who has experienced both, write a letter to a younger student either agreeing or disagreeing with this statement.

- You sit down at the lunch table with three interesting friends who have a running bet concerning the person with the most embarrassing moment. You drop your backpack, stand up and declare yourself the winner. Write the narrative that you told your friends that day to win the contest.

- Write about a moment in your life when choosing to be honest was a difficult choice. Describe the dilemma and how you made your decision to do the right thing.

- Imagine that the time is late at night. You or a character in your story is at home or in a familiar place when the telephone rings. Create a story that includes this scene.

- Imagine that you are caring for younger children for an evening. Make up a story to tell them to entertain them. Create a new story rather than using one that you have heard before.

- Sometimes things turn out in a way you do not think will happen. Tell about a time or event that turned out differently than you expected.

- Think about a time when you, another person, or some situation challenged you in some way. Tell what happened.

informative essay prompts

- Think of the most valuable thing you own that was not purchased at a store. Write to a friend explaining why the item is so important to you and how your life would be changed without this item.

- Imagine you have been asked during middle school registration at your elementary school to write an entertaining speech entitled, "How to Survive a Day in the Life of a Middle School Student." What would you say?

- Your class has a substitute teacher, and you have been chosen to be the substitute's "Teacher Aide" for the day. Your first job is to clearly explain the daily routine and assignments for the class as well as behavioral expectations.

- Inventions are all around us. Choose one invention and report to your teacher explaining the positive and or negative impact of this invention on teenagers.
- You have been asked to write an introductory essay for the upcoming freshman survival guide advising incoming ninth grade students in areas of school and social life.
- Choose a person in your life whom you admire. Write a story about that person, explaining why you admire them.
- You have been asked to choose one item that will show what life is like in our present day society. The item will be placed in a time capsule to be opened in two hundred years. Explain what item you choose and why.
- Children have a special position in their family. Explain the advantages and disadvantages of the position you hold in your family—youngest child, only child, middle child, oldest child, etc.
- Choose a character from a story or book you have read this year. Describe one of his or her qualities and use evidence from the story to support the quality you choose.
- How does city life differ from rural? Use your experience as well as insights gained in class to write your essay.

persuasive essay prompts

- Chewing gum in school is against the rules. Write a letter to your principal explaining why this rule should be eliminated.
- To ensure the safety of park users, city officials are considering a bill that would ban skateboarding and in-line skating in public parks areas not designated for such use. Write a letter to your city councilman stating whether you agree or disagree with this proposal.
- Write an essay that demonstrates whether you agree or disagree with the following statement:

  The use of affirmative action as a means of setting quotas for employment, admission to educational institutions, and the awarding of government contracts is in and of itself discriminatory and should therefore be revoked as a public program.

- In order to help maintain discipline and avoid "fashion competition," your school administrators intend to revise your school's dress code to include school uniforms as part of the dress code. Write a letter to your school principal, persuading him against his plan.
- Write an essay that clearly presents your response to the following: The death penalty is both "cruel" and "unusual" and a violation of the eighth amendment to the Constitution of the United States.
- The management of your favorite shopping mall plans to institute a policy whereby juveniles under the age of sixteen (16) years of age must be accompanied by a parent, guardian, or responsible adult after the hour of six P.M. They have requested public reaction to their plan. Write a letter telling the mall's management whether you agree or disagree.
- Your parents have decided you may only watch one hour of TV on school nights. In a well-organized composition decide whether or not you agree with their decision and why. Persuade your parents as to how long you feel you should be allowed to watch TV. Be sure to state and support at least two premises (reasons) for your opinion.
- Your parents promised you that you could have a friend spend the night on the weekend. Now they have changed their minds because they must leave town, and they do not want to leave you unsupervised. Persuade them to change their minds again and let your friend stay the night.
- The recent legislature passed a law that banned all tobacco products from school buildings and grounds. Take a stand about this new law and try to persuade your reader to see the situation from your point of view.
- Pretend that a friend of yours has decided not to eat milk, cheese, or vegetables of any kind. Write an essay to your friend explaining the dietary harm of her plan. Use good reasons to convince your friend.
- You will be dissecting frogs in your science class. Some of your friends are opposed, considering it cruelty to animals. Are you for or against them? Take a stand. Write a letter for or against the planned frog dissection.